Monkeysuits

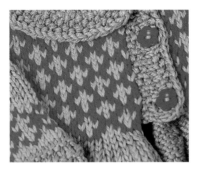

Monkeysuits

Sweaters
& More
to Knit
for Kids

SHARON TURNER

The Taunton Press

The Taunton Press
Inspiration for hands-on living™

The Taunton Press, Inc., 63 South Main Street, PO Box 5506, Newtown, CT 06470-5506
e-mail: tp@taunton.com

Distributed by Publishers Group West

COVER DESIGN: Ann Marie Manca
INTERIOR DESIGN AND LAYOUT: Cathy Cassidy
ILLUSTRATOR: Rosalie Vaccaro
PHOTOGRAPHER: Jack Deutsch

LIBRARY OF CONGRESS CATALOGING-IN-PUBLICATION DATA:
Turner, Sharon.
    Monkeysuits : sweaters & more to knit for kids / Sharon Turner.
        p. cm.
    ISBN 1-56158-493-2
     1. Knitting--Patterns. 2. Children's clothing. 3. Sweaters. I. Title.
TT825 .T87 2001
746.43'2041--dc21   2001033101

Printed in the United States of America
10 9 8 7 6 5 4 3 2 1

To my family (and that means all of you!)

ACKNOWLEDGMENTS

First and foremost, my thanks go to Sarah Coe at Taunton Press for asking whether I was interested in doing a book. The project simply wouldn't have happened without her vision, dedication, and humor. I am also grateful to:

My daughters, Isabel and Matilda, who inspired me to design and knit in the first place.

My husband, Mark Paul, who has been my business partner, photographer, Web site designer, pattern namer, color adviser, and a million other things.

My sister, Doll, and my brother-in-law, Ken, for their unceasing enthusiasm and wise counsel and for Doll's endless supply of new ideas.

My mother-in-law, Sue Paul, who has tied yarn onto thousands of pattern cards and who is a saint.

My Dad, Tony Turner, who put me through art school, my stepmother, Carol Turner, and all of the other family members and friends who have kindly given help and encouragement or have offered their children as models for the original patterns.

My father-in-law, Doug Paul, and my nephew and nieces, Turner, Liz, and Anna, for tying yarn onto the cards that Sue didn't do and for helping me with mailings and numerous photo shoots.

All of the adorable models, Olivia Moss Binzen, Mikayla Cubbege, Matthew Conklin, Hannah Delohery, Rosamund Sarah Elizabeth Deutsch-Kirkup, Griffin Liebel, Skylar Rose Mandell, Isabel Paul, Matilda Paul, Cameron Phillips, Tommy Rahr, Benjamin Roman, and William Roman, who posed for this book and looked so cute, and their parents, for generously giving their time and children to the project.

The photographer, Jack Deutsch, for getting the kids to smile and look natural in a not-so-natural setting.

Deb Surprenant, for her careful copyediting, and all of the people at Taunton Press who have been working behind the scenes to complete the book and make it look so good.

All of the knitters and shop owners who have been so supportive of Monkeysuits along the way.

p. 4   p. 10   p. 16   p. 22   p. 28   p. 36

CONTENTS

p. 42   p. 50   p. 56   p. 62   p. 68   p. 74

p. 80   p. 86   p. 92   p. 98   p. 104   p. 110

p. 116   p. 122   p. 128   p. 134   p. 140   p. 146

INTRODUCTION

I knit my first baby sweater when I was pregnant with my daughter Isabel. I had been knitting on and off in spurts for years, usually starting projects and never finishing them, or finishing them and not being happy with the results. When I finished that baby sweater—it was a moss stitch cardigan from an old Pingouin pattern—I experienced for the first time true, complete satisfaction with something I had knit. I was hooked. During Isabel's first year, I must have knit 15 sweaters for her, plus sweaters as baby gifts for others. It was easy to experiment with new designs since the sweaters were so small and knit up so quickly. The interval between inspiration and completion was so short that momentum was never lost. (And ripping out wasn't as daunting as it had been on adult sweaters.)

As Isabel's pile of sweaters grew, my sister and my husband encouraged me to publish the designs as pattern leaflets, which is how Monkeysuits got started.

The first few Monkeysuits were primarily for infants and toddlers, but as my children have grown, so has the size range. Many of the outfits in this book go up in size to 12 years, and a few can be knit for adults. The skill level varies from pattern to pattern, as do the yarn weights, so there should be something for every knitter. The generic gauge is listed for yarns used, so if you can't find the yarn specified for a particular pattern, you can easily substitute it with another type of yarn. I hope that you will enjoy knitting up some of these sweaters for the little "monkeys" in your life. There is no gift like a hand-knit sweater—it has the maker's affection for the wearer woven into the fabric.

ABBREVIATIONS

alt	alternate	p2tog	purl 2 stitches together
approx	approximately	patt	pattern
beg	begin(ning)	pm	place marker
bet	between	psso	pass slipped stitch over
BO	bind off	pu	pick up
CC	contrast color	rem	remain(ing)(s)
ch	chain	rep	repeat
circ	circular	rev	reverse
cm	centimeter(s)	rnd(s)	round(s)
cn	cable needle	RS(s)	right side(s)
CO	cast on	RSS	reverse stockinette stitch
cont	continue	sc	single crochet
dc	double crochet	sep	separate
dec	decrease	skp	slip 1, knit 1, pass slipped stitch over
dpn(s)	double-pointed needle(s)	sl	slip
g st	garter stitch	ssk	slip 1 stitch as if to knit, slip another stitch as if to knit, then knit these 2 stitches together
in.	inch(es)		
inc	increase		
k	knit	st(s)	stitch(es)
k2tog	knit 2 stitches together	st st	stockinette stitch
m1	make 1 by picking up horizontal loop before next stitch and knitting into the back of it	tbl	through back of loop(s)
		tog	together
		WS(s)	wrong side(s)
MC	main color	wyib	with yarn in back
oz.	ounce(s)	wyif	with yarn in front
p	purl	yo	yarn over

JACKY-O

The name says it all. This set consists of
a classic jacket knit in a linen stitch pattern,
which creates a wonderful woven-looking fabric,
and a matching pillbox hat. The linen stitch looks good
on the right side and the wrong side, so if the sleeves
need to be rolled up, it's not a disaster. In retrospect,
I think I should have designed a skirt to go with this set.
It wouldn't be difficult to do. You could work up
a big tube, fold the top edge inside, and insert an elastic
waistband. Though this set is knit in cotton, it
would also work well in wool.

JACKY-O

Linen Stitch Jacket and Pillbox Hat

∴ **MATERIALS**

Jacket

8 (10, 11, 12, 14) 50g balls Classic Elite Newport (100% cotton, 70 yd./64m per ball) in Baroque Tint #2089 (A) and 1 ball in black #2013 (B), or chunky yarn that will knit to gauge given below
Size 10 ½ (7mm) knitting needles or size needed to match linen st gauge given below
Four stitch holders, row counter, tapestry needle, markers
Nine ¾-in. buttons to match B

Hat

1 (2, 2) balls A, 1 ball B
Size 6 (4mm) knitting needles
Size 8 (5mm) knitting needles or size needed to match hat gauge given below

Set

9 (11, 12, 14, 15) balls A, 2 balls B

∴ **SIZES**

2–3 (4–5, 6–7, 8–9, 10–12) years
Length: 13½ (14½, 15½, 16½, 17½) in.
Chest: 24 (26, 28, 30, 32) in.
Sleeve: 10½ (11½, 12½, 13½, 14½) in.
Hat circumference: S-18½ (M-20, L-22) in.

∴ **GAUGE**

Generic yarn gauge: 16 sts and 22 rows to 4 in./10cm over st st on size 9 (5.5mm) needles
Linen st gauge: 22 sts and 30 rows to 4 in./10cm on size 10½ needles
Hat gauge: 18 sts and 24 rows to 4 in./10cm over st st on size 8 (5mm) needles
Don't waste precious time and precious yarn—make a gauge swatch before beginning!

∴ **PATTERN STITCH**

Linen st (multiple of 2 sts plus 1)
Row 1 (RS): *K1, sl 1 st purlwise wyif, bring yarn to back of work*; rep from * to * to last st, k1.
Row 2: P1, *p1, sl 1 st purlwise wyib, bring yarn to front of work*; rep from * to * to last 2 sts, end p2.

JACKET

Back

With size 10½ needles and A, CO 77 (83, 89, 93, 99) sts. Beg with a RS row, work linen st for 7½ (8, 8½, 9, 9½) in.

Shape armhole: BO 6 sts beg next 2 rows, maintaining patt—65 (71, 77, 81, 87) sts. Cont without further shaping until back measures 13½ (14½, 15½, 16½, 17½) in., ending with a WS row.

Next row: Patt across first 19 (21, 23, 23, 25) sts, join second ball, and BO center 27 (29, 31, 35, 37) sts, patt across rem 19 (21, 23, 23, 25) sts.

Next row (WS): BO both sets of shoulder sts.

Pocket flaps (make four alike)

With size 10½ needles and A, CO 19 (21, 23, 25, 25) sts. Beg with a RS row, work linen st for 9 (9, 11, 11, 11) rows. Leave sts on holders.

Left front

With size 10½ needles and A, CO 43 (47, 49, 53, 55) sts. Beg with a RS row, work in linen st for 3½ (3¾, 4, 4¼, 4½) in., ending with a RS row.

Next row (WS): Patt across first 13 (13, 13, 15, 15) sts, and then BO 19 (21, 23, 25, 25) sts in patt, patt across rem 11 (13, 13, 13, 15) sts.

Next row (RS)—attach pocket flap: Patt across first 11 (13, 13, 13, 15) sts. Then cont in patt across the 19 (21, 23, 25, 25) sts of one of the pocket flaps, with RS up, in place of the bound-off sts, patt to end.
Cont in patt until piece measures 7½ (8, 8½, 9, 9½) in. from beg, ending with a WS row.

Shape armhole: BO 6 sts beg next row—37 (41, 43, 47, 49) sts.
Cont without shaping until piece measures 9¾ (10¾, 11½, 12¼, 13) in. from beg, ending with a RS row.

Next row (WS): Patt across first 13 (13, 13, 15, 15) sts, and BO 19 (21, 23, 25, 25) sts in patt. Then patt across rem 5 (7, 7, 7, 9) sts.

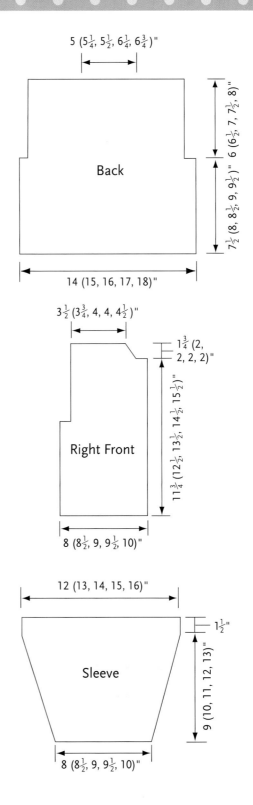

5 (5¼, 5½, 6¼, 6¾)"

Back

6 (6½, 7, 7½, 8)"

7½ (8, 8½, 9, 9½)"

14 (15, 16, 17, 18)"

3½ (3¾, 4, 4, 4½)"

1¾ (2, 2, 2, 2)"

Right Front

11¾ (12½, 13½, 14½, 15½)"

8 (8½, 9, 9½, 10)"

12 (13, 14, 15, 16)"

1½"

Sleeve

9 (10, 11, 12, 13)"

8 (8½, 9, 9½, 10)"

Next row (RS)—attach pocket flap: Patt across first 5 (7, 7, 7, 9) sts; then cont in patt across the 19 (21, 23, 25, 25) sts of the second pocket flap in place of the bound-off sts, patt to end.

Cont in patt until left front measures 11¾ (12½, 13½, 14½, 15½) in. from beg, ending with a RS row.

Next row (WS)—shape neck: BO first 8 (8, 8, 10, 10) sts; work to end.

Then dec 1 st at neck edge every row (by k2tog on RS, p2tog on WS), maintaining patt, until 19 (21, 23, 23, 25) sts rem.

Work without further shaping until left front measures same as back. BO sts. Place five markers for buttons—1½ in. up from bottom, ½ in. down from neck edge, and three more evenly spaced bet those two.

Right front

Work as for left front until piece measures 1½ in., ending with a WS row.

Next row (RS)—work first buttonhole: Patt 2, k2tog, yo, patt to end.

Cont as set, working right front as for left front, working buttonholes opposite markers as established, reversing armhole and neck shaping, and placing pocket flaps as follows: When right front measures 3½ (3¾, 4, 4¼, 4½) in. from beg and you are ready to begin a WS row, patt across first 11 (13, 13, 13, 15) sts, and then BO 19 (21, 23, 25, 25) sts in patt, patt across rem 13 (13, 13, 15, 15) sts.

Next row (RS)—attach pocket flap: Patt across first 13 (13, 13, 15, 15) sts. Cont in patt across the 19 (21, 23, 25, 25) sts of one of the pocket flaps, with RS up, in place of the bound-off sts, patt to end.

To place breast pocket flap, work until right front measures 9¾ (10¾, 11½, 12¼, 13) in. from beg, ending with a RS row.

Next row (WS): Patt across first 5 (7, 7, 7, 9) sts, BO 19 (21, 23, 25, 25) sts in patt, and then patt across rem 13 (13, 13, 15, 15) sts.

Next row (RS)—attach pocket flap: Patt across first 13 (13, 13, 15, 15) sts, and then cont in patt across the 19 (21, 23, 25, 25) sts of the second pocket flap in place of the bound-off sts, patt to end.

Sleeves

With size 10½ needles and A, CO 45 (47, 49, 53, 55) sts. Work 2 rows in linen st.

Next row (RS): Inc 1 st each end this row. Then dec 1 st each end every fourth row 4 (4, 6, 6, 8) times, and then every sixth row 6 (7, 7, 8, 8) times to 67 (71, 77, 83, 89) sts, maintaining patt changes at beg and end of rows.

Work without further shaping until sleeve measures 10½ (11½, 12½, 13½, 14½) in. BO sts, leaving a tail twice the width of sleeve top to sew sleeve to body.

> ### tip
> If substituting yarn, go by the generic gauge when purchasing. Linen st is unusual in that it requires a needle size larger than the yarn calls for to reach a smaller gauge than the yarn usually knits to.

Finishing

Weave in loose ends, except those you will use to sew seams. Sew shoulder seams. Steam all pieces and shoulder seams.

Attach sleeves: Center sleeve on armhole with RSs facing each other, and pin in place. Backstitch sleeve top to armhole edge, sewing the bound-off sts at armhole edges to the straight side edge at top of sleeve. Sew inside sleeve and side seams. Steam.

Crocheted edgings: With size H crochet hook and B, and beg on RS at left side seam, sc across back CO edge. (Make sure crocheted edge is not distorting the hem. If it's too tight, try a larger hook. If it's causing the hem to flare and stretch, try a smaller hook, or try skipping a stitch every few stitches.) Cont across right front CO edge, up right front edge and around neck, down left front edge, and around left front CO edge to where you began. Without turning, work a second row of sc all around. Cut yarn, pull through last loop, and weave in ends. Work one row of sc in B around the three open edges of all pocket flaps. Work two rows sc in B around cuffs.

Whipstitch bound-off edges of pocket holes to back of top of pocket flaps. Sew buttons to pocket flaps, going all the way through the jacket to hold the flap down. Sew the rem five buttons opposite the buttonholes.

PILLBOX HAT

With size 6 needle and B, CO 80 (90, 100) sts. K 4 rows.

Next row (RS): Change to A and size 8 needles, and beg with a k row. Work in st st until piece measures 3¾ (4¼, 4¾) in. from beg, ending with a WS row.
Change to B, and k five rows.

Next row (WS): Change back to A, and p this row.

Starting with next row, shape crown as follows:

Row 1: *K2tog, k6 (7, 8)*; rep from * to * across—70 (80, 90) sts.

Row 2 and all WS rows unless otherwise indicated: P even.

Row 3: *K2tog, k5 (6, 7)*; rep from * to * across—60 (70, 80) sts.

Row 5: *K2tog, k4 (5, 6)*; rep from * to * across—50 (60, 70) sts.
Cont shaping crown as established, decreasing 10 sts every RS row, evenly spaced, until 20 sts rem—11 (13, 15) rows total.

Next row (WS): P.

Next row: K2tog across row—10 sts.

Next row (WS): P2tog across—5 sts.
Cut yarn, leaving a long enough tail to sew crown seam. Pull yarn through rem 5 sts, tighten, and secure. Sew crown and back seams. Weave in loose ends.

GET SHORTY

This set was inspired by a crude illustration of a clown
that I saw in a children's book. He was wearing huge navy
and light blue checked trousers held up by suspenders
with big yellow buttons. I had been thinking about
designing something similar to German lederhosen—which
I dearly wanted myself when I was about 7—and the check
pattern seemed just the thing. When I finished them,
I asked my husband what I should call them,
and he said, "Get Shorty." Both the shorts and the hat
are knit using bobbins and the intarsia method,
but the separations are straight lines, so there is really
nothing to it. Though the original shorts you see here
are knit in cotton, several knitters have made these
in wool for a dressy winter outfit.

GET SHORTY

Unisex Checked Shorts with Suspenders and Matching Beanie

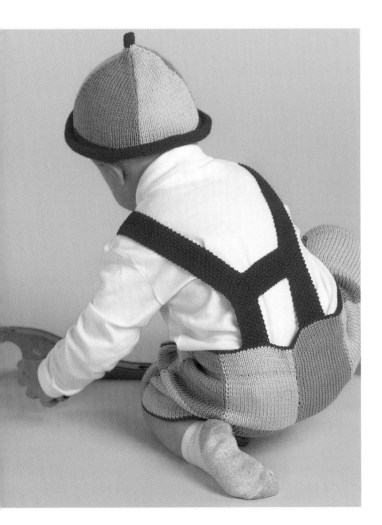

⋮ MATERIALS

Shorts

1 (2, 2, 2, 3) 50g skein each Dale of Norway Kolibri cotton (114 yd./105m per skein) in blue #5824 (A), yellow #2017 (B), and 1 (2, 2, 2, 2) skein red #3808 (C), or yarn that will knit to the gauge given below
Two 1¼-in. green buttons
Size 3 (3.25mm) knitting needles
Size 5 (3.75mm) knitting needles or size needed to match gauge given below
Eight yarn bobbins

Beanie

1 (1, 1, 1, 1) skein each A, B, and C
Size 5 knitting needles
Set of size 5 dpns
Four yarn bobbins

Set

2 (2, 2, 3, 3) skeins each blue, yellow, and red

⋮ SIZES

6 months (1, 2, 3–4, 5–6 years)
Length: 13½ (15, 17, 19, 20½) in.
Waist (loose fit): 20 (21, 22½, 24, 24½) in.
Hat circumference: S-15½ (M-17, L-18½, XL-20) in.

⋮ GAUGE

24 sts and 30 rows to 4 in./10cm in st st on size 5 needles
Don't waste precious time and precious yarn—make a gauge swatch before beginning!

⋮ PATTERN STITCHES

Seed st (for suspenders)

> **Row 1:** *K1, p1*; rep from * to * to end of row.

> **Row 2:** *P1, k1*; rep from * to * to end of row.
> Repeat these two rows for seed st.

Two-row horizontal buttonhole (over 7 sts)

> **Row 1:** Work to the placement of the buttonhole as indicated, k2. With left needle, pull the first st

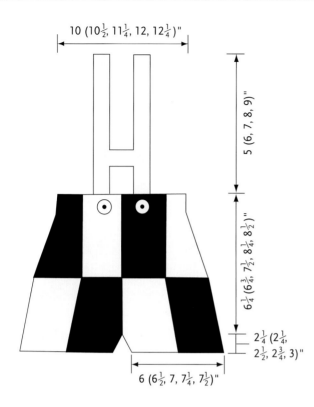

10 (10½, 11¼, 12, 12¼)"

5 (6, 7, 8, 9)"

6¼ (6¾, 7½, 8¼, 8½)"

2¼ (2¼, 2½, 2¾, 3)"

6 (6½, 7, 7¼, 7½)"

over the second, *k1, pull the second st over the newer k st*; rep from * to * five times more (7 sts bound off).

Row 2: Work to the bound-off sts, CO 7 sts, work to end of row.

Row 3: K the CO sts tbl to tighten them.

One-row horizontal buttonhole (more difficult, but neater, also over 7 sts)

Row 1: Work to placement of buttonhole as indicated. Bring yarn to front, and sl 1 st purlwise. Bring yarn to back, and drop it. *Sl next st from left needle to right needle. Pass the first sl st over it*. Rep from * to * six times more, keeping yarn at back. Sl last bound-off st back to left needle, and turn work.

Row 2: CO 8 sts (one more than you bound off) using cable CO method: Holding yarn at back, *insert right needle bet first and second sts on left needle. Bring up a loop, and put it onto the left needle as you would when doing a k CO*. Rep from * to * seven times more. Turn work.

Row 3: Holding yarn at back, sl first st from left needle to right, and bring the extra CO st over it to complete the buttonhole. Work to end. This buttonhole needs no reinforcement.

SHORTS

Legs (make two)

Before you begin, wind 4 bobbins each A and B. With size 3 needles and C, CO 88 (96, 102, 108, 114) sts. Work 1 in. in st st, ending with a WS row.
P 1 row for turning hem.
Begin color blocks (WS)—change to larger needles and a bobbin of B. P26 (28, 30, 32, 34), change to A, p18 (20, 21, 22, 23), change to second bobbin B, p18 (20, 21, 22, 23), change to second bobbin A, p26 (28, 30, 32, 34). Take care to twist yarns on WS of work when changing color to prevent holes.

Next row (RS): K26 (28, 30, 32, 34) A, k18 (20, 21, 22, 23) B, k18 (20, 21, 22, 23) A, k26 (28, 30, 32, 34) B.
Cont in this manner, maintaining colors as set for 2¼ (2¼, 2½, 2¾, 3) in. above turning row.
BO 4 (4, 5, 5, 6) sts beg next 2 rows.
BO 2 (2, 2, 3, 3) sts beg next 2 rows; then dec 1 st beg next 4 rows—72 (80, 84, 88, 92) sts.

Body

Sl sts from both legs onto same needle. Work as one piece, joining legs at center front—144 (160, 168, 176, 184) sts. Cont with colors as set until piece measures 4¼ (4½, 5, 5½, 5¾) in. above turning row, ending with a WS row (end of first row of checks). Change color blocks as follows:

Row 1 (RS): *K18 (20, 21, 22, 23) B, k18 (20, 21, 22, 23) A*; rep from * to * three times.

Row 2: *P18 (20, 21, 22, 23) A, p18 (20, 21, 22, 23) B*; rep from * to * three times.

Row 3: Work as for first row.

Begin shaping waist—fourth row (WS): *P18 (20, 21, 22, 23) A, p16 (18, 19, 20, 21), p2tog B; p2tog tbl, p16 (18, 19, 20, 21) A; p18 (20, 21, 22, 23) B*. Rep from * to * once.

Cont in this manner, maintaining colors and decreasing 4 sts per row as set (see tip for RS row dec method at right), every fourth row 2 (0, 3, 5, 4) times, and then every third row 3 (7, 4, 2, 4) times to 120 (128, 136, 144, 148) sts.

Having completed shaping, work until piece measures 7¾ (8¼, 9¼, 10¼, 10¾) in. above turn-

ing row. Then make two buttonholes—one each centered on the two center front checks (fourth and fifth color blocks). Work buttonholes on RS row, still maintaining color changes, using one of the two methods described in "Pattern Stitches": K48 (51, 54, 58, 60), work buttonhole, k10 (12, 14, 14, 14), work buttonhole, k rem 48 (51, 54, 58, 60) sts.

Cont with patt as set until piece measures 8½ (9, 10, 11, 11½) in., ending with a WS row.

Hem at waist

Change to C and smaller needles. K two rows (second row will be for turning hem).

Next row (RS): Begin st st in C only, and work until hem measures ¾ in. from turning row at waist, ending with WS row.

Work buttonholes: Make buttonholes as you did before—k48 (51, 54, 58, 60), work buttonhole, k10 (12, 14, 14, 14), work buttonhole, k rem 48 (51, 54, 58, 60) sts.

Cont in st st until hem measures 1¼ in.; BO.

Suspenders (make two)

With size 3 needles and C, CO 10 sts. Work in seed st until suspender measures 12 (14, 16, 18, 20) in. long; BO.

Cross brace (for holding suspenders together at back): With size 3 needles and C, CO 10 sts. Work in seed st to 1½ (2, 2, 2½, 2½) in.; BO.

Finishing

Weave in loose ends. Lay piece flat on ironing board,
cover with a light cotton cloth, and lightly steam press
with hems on legs and waist turned under. Sew back
seam. Sew crotch seams. Pin and whipstitch leg hem
and waistband in place, taking care to line up buttonholes. Sew inside leg seams. Neatly stitch the buttonhole fronts and backs tog, using the same color yarn
as the square in which the buttonhole is placed. Sew
one end of each suspender to back along inside waistband ¾ (1, 1, 1¼, 1¼) in. away from center back seam
on each side. Sew cross brace to inside edges of suspenders 1½ (2, 2½, 3, 3½) in. up from waistband. Sew
buttons to ends of suspenders using yellow yarn
(separated into a few ply) as thread.

BEANIE

Make 2 bobbins each A and B.

Rolled brim: With size 5 needles and C, CO 112 (124,
134, 142) sts. Beg with a k row, work 2 in. in st st,
ending with a RS row.

   Next row (WS): Dec 20 (20, 22, 22) sts evenly
   across row to 92 (104, 112, 120) sts.

Begin color-block segments (RS):
*K23 (26, 28, 30) A, k23 (26, 28, 30)
B*; rep from * to * once.

Next row (WS): *P23 (26, 28, 30)
B, p23 (26, 28, 30) A*; rep from
* to * once.
Repeat these 2 rows 5 (7, 9, 11)
times more.

Next row (RS): *Using A, skp, k19
(22, 24, 26), k2tog; change to B,
skp, k19 (22, 24, 26), k2tog*; rep
from * to * once.
Work 3 rows even with colors as set.

Next row (RS): *Using A, skp, k17 (20, 22, 24),
k2tog; change to B, skp, k17 (20, 22, 24), k2tog*;
rep from * to * once.
Work 3 rows even.
Cont from here to dec 8 sts as set every RS row
until 20 (16, 16, 16) sts remain.

Next row (WS): Work even.

Next row (RS): *Using A, skp, k3 (2,2,2) tog;
change to B, skp, k3 (2, 2, 2) tog*; rep from
* to * once.
Change to C and p one row. Put rem 8 sts onto
dpn and k8.
*Slide sts to opposite end of dpn to work next row
as a RS row, k8*. Rep from * to * for ½ in.
BO, pull yarn through center of stem, and secure.

Finishing

Weave in loose ends. Sew back seam, reversing at
rolled edge.

PUPPY LOVE

My daughter Matilda, who is very playful and cuddly,
inspired this set when she was in the crawling phase.
She acted so much like a puppy that we thought
she should dress like one too. This sweater and hat
is for babies 3 months to 2 years, but the sweater
is generously sized, so you should get a few
years of wear out of it. Worked in a combination
of garter stitch and stockinette stitch, it's very easy
to make and a good project for someone
new to knitting. And like Yellow Jacket (p. 86),
this set can be worn as a Halloween costume.

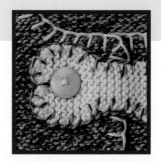

PUPPY LOVE

Cardigan with Dog-Bone Tab Closures and Matching Dog-Eared Bonnet

Cardigan

2 (2, 2, 2) 100g skeins Cascade 220 (100% wool, 220 yd. per ball) in gray tweed #9402 (MC) and 1 skein natural white #8010 (CC), or other worsted weight yarn that will knit to gauge given below
Size 8 (5mm) knitting needles or size needed to match gauge given below
Three size 8 dpns
Four stitch holders, tapestry needle
Four ⅞-in. to 1-in. buttons
One large snap

Hat

One skein each MC and CC
Two ⅝-in. buttons
Size 6 (4mm) knitting needles
Size 8 (5mm) knitting needles or size needed to match gauge given below

Set

2 (3, 3, 3) skeins MC and 1 skein CC

∵ SIZES

Sweater: 3–6 (6–9, 9–12, 12–24) months
Length: 10 (10½, 11, 12) in.
Chest: 22 (24, 26, 28) in.
Sleeve: 5 (5½, 6½, 7½) in. with cuff turned back
Hat sizes: 3–6 (6–9, 9–12, 12–24) months

∵ GAUGE

18 sts and 24 rows to 4 in./10cm over st st on size 8 (5mm) needles
Don't waste precious time and precious yarn—make a gauge swatch before beginning!

CARDIGAN

Back

With size 8 needles and MC, CO 49 (54, 58, 63) sts. Work in g st (k every row) for 2 in., ending with a RS row. Beg with a p row, work remainder of back in st st until back measures 10 (10½, 11, 12) in. from beg.

Next row: Work across first 16 (18, 19, 21) sts, and put on holder for later. BO center 17 (18, 20, 21) sts for neck, patt across rem 16 (18, 19, 21) sts, and put on second holder.

Right front (worked in g st entirely)

With size 8 needles and MC, CO 29 (31, 34, 36) sts. Work in g st until piece measures 9 (9, 9½, 10½) in. from beg, ending with a WS row.

Shape neck: BO first 10 (10, 12, 12) sts, and work to end. Work WS even.

Next row (RS): Dec 1 st beg this row, and then 1 st beg next 2 RS rows to 16 (18, 19, 21) sts. Work without further shaping until piece measures same as back, and put sts onto holder for later.

Left front

Work as for right front, reversing neck shaping.

Sleeves

With size 8 needle and MC, CO 27 (29, 31, 34) sts. Work in g st for 2½ in., ending with a WS row.
Beg with a k row, work remainder of sleeve in st st and increase 1 st each end this row, then every fourth row 7 (6, 3, 0) times, then every sixth row 0 (1, 4, 7) times to 43 (45, 47, 50) sts.
Cont without further shaping until sleeve measures 7½ (8, 9, 10) in. from beg. BO sts, leaving a tail twice the length of the width of sleeve top to sew sleeve to sweater later.

Dog-bone tab enclosures
(make two alike—worked entirely in g st)

With size 8 needle and CC, CO on 5 sts. K 1 row. Inc 1 st each end next row, and then every other row 2 more times to 11 sts. K 5 rows even.

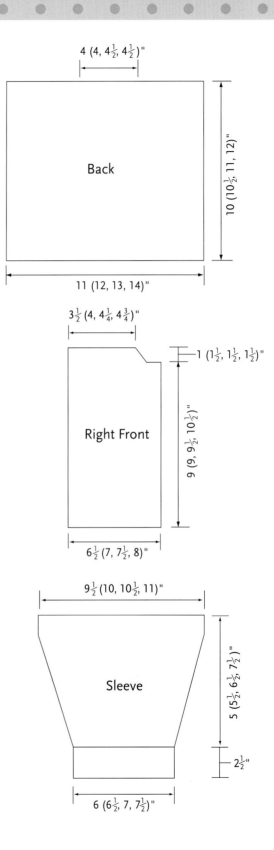

4 (4, 4½, 4½)"

Back

10 (10½, 11, 12)"

11 (12, 13, 14)"

3½ (4, 4¼, 4¾)"

1 (1½, 1½, 1½)"

Right Front

9 (9, 9½, 10½)"

6½ (7, 7½, 8)"

9½ (10, 10½, 11)"

Sleeve

5 (5½, 6½, 7½)"

2½"

6 (6½, 7, 7½)"

Buttonhole row: K5, yo, k2tog, k4. K five rows even.

Next row: Ssk, k across to last 2 sts, k2tog.

Next row: K.
Rep last two rows one more time to 7 sts. Work in g st without further shaping until bone measures 3½ in. from beg. Inc 1 st each end next row, and then 1 st each end every other row 1 more time to 11 sts. K 5 rows. Work buttonhole as before on next row. K 5 rows.

Next row: Ssk, k across to last 2 sts, k2tog.

Next row: K.
Rep last two rows two more times to 5 sts; BO last row.
Take a strand of CC threaded into a tapestry needle. Make the circular ends of the tab closures look less like barbells and more like bones by inserting the needle about ½ in. in from CO or bound-off edge and wrapping tightly around the edge, reinserting the needle a few times to pinch in the outside edges of the circles.
Work blanket st around perimeters of tabs in MC.

Finishing

Use the BO seam technique for shoulder seams as follows: With RSs facing each other, place the sts from the left front and back shoulder each onto a size 8 dpn, and hold the needles parallel. Insert a third dpn into the first st on the first needle as if to k, then into the first st on the second needle as if to k, and k the two sts as one. Repeat this a second time—there should now be 2 sts on the right needle. *Pass the first st on the right needle over the second and BO*. K the next 2 sts on the parallel dpn together, and rep from * to *. Cont in this way, knitting the corresponding sts of each shoulder together and binding off as you go, until 1 st remains on the right needle. Break yarn, and pull through last st to secure. Repeat this process for right shoulder. Weave in loose ends, except for those that will be used to sew seams. Lightly steam pieces to block, including shoulder seams.

Attach sleeves: Center sleeve on armhole with RSs facing each other, and backstitch sleeve top to armhole edge. Sew sleeve and side seams, and lightly steam.
Work blanket st in CC around edges of entire sweater, including cuffs. Sew snap to neck edge, creating about a 1-in. overlap of fronts. Snap sweater, lay flat, and place one dog-bone tab closure across front, centered under the neck, about ½ in. below neck shaping. Sew two buttons where holes lie using CC threaded into needle. Place second dog-bone tab about 1 in. below bottom edge of first, and sew rem two buttons.

HAT

Ears (make two alike— worked entirely in g st)

With size 8 needles and CC, CO 5 sts. K one row. Inc 1 st each end next row, and then every other row 3 more times to 13 sts. Work without further shaping to 3½ in. Put sts onto holder.

Hat body

With size 6 needle and MC, CO 50 (52, 56, 58) sts. Work for ¾ in. in g st. Change to size 8 needles, and cont working g st until piece measures 5 (5½, 6, 6½) in. from beg, ending with a WS row.

Attach ears: K3, then holding first ear sts on a dpn parallel to needle holding hat sts, k the hat and ear together by inserting needle into first ear st on dpn as if to k, and then into next hat st as if to k, and k these two sts as one. Rep this process across rem ear sts. K across next 18 (20, 24, 26) sts. Attach second ear in the same manner as first across next 13 sts; k rem 3 sts. K next WS row.

Shape top: K32 (33, 36, 37), k2tog tbl, turn.

Next row (WS): Sl 1 st as if to p, p14 (14, 16, 16), p2tog, turn.

Next row (RS): Sl 1 st as if to p, k14 (14, 16, 16), k2tog tbl, turn.
Rep last 2 rows until only center 16 (16, 18, 18) sts rem. Leave these sts on holder or needle.

Edging: With size 6 needle and MC, starting at right front bottom corner with RS facing, pick up and k 23 (25, 27, 29) sts up side to held sts. K across held 16 (16, 18, 18) sts, pick up and k 23 (25, 27, 29) sts down to left front bottom corner—62 (66, 72, 76) sts total. K 8 rows, binding off on last row. Weave in all loose ends.

Chin strap (worked entirely in g st)

With size 6 needle and CC, CO 3 sts. K one row. Inc 1 st each end next row, and then every other row two more times to 9 sts. K two rows even.

Buttonhole row: K4, yo, k2tog, k3.
K two rows even.

Next row: Ssk, k5, k2tog.

Next row: K row even.

Next row: Ssk, k3, k2tog—5 sts.
Cont working without further shaping for an additional 2 in.

Next row: Inc 1 st each end of row.
Then inc 1 st each end every other row one more time to 9 sts. K two rows even.

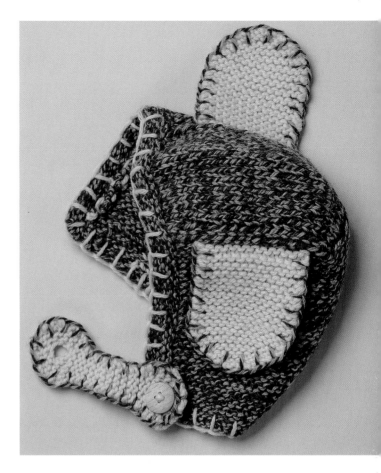

Buttonhole row: Work as before.
K two more rows even.

Next row: Ssk, k5, k2tog.

Next row: K even.

Next row: Ssk, k3, k2tog.

Next row: K even.

Next row: Ssk, k1, k2tog—3 sts.; BO sts.

Finishing

Weave in ends. Work blanket st in CC around all edges of hat. Work blanket st in MC around edges of ears and chin strap. Sew one button to each corner of hat, and button chin strap.

VESTED INTEREST

Vests are an excellent layering option. They're great for keeping little ones warm while allowing them to move freely. Vests with buttons have a dressier look, and this vest, a pullover, is great for everyday. This was the first Monkeysuit to go past size 6. My sister's kids are older than mine, and I wanted to make something for my then 10-year-old niece Anna. She dresses simply, so I didn't want to make anything too baroque. This vest, in the larger size of course, ended up being a wardrobe staple for Anna, who flattered me and wore hers into the ground. My version is knit in cotton, but it would be fine in wool as well.

VESTED INTEREST

Unisex Cropped Striped Cotton Vest with Matching Hat

⁛ MATERIALS

Vest

2 (2, 3, 3, 4, 4) 50g balls Rowan HandKnit DK Cotton (90 yd./85m per ball) in Sunkissed #231 (A), 1 (1, 1, 2, 2, 2) ball in Soft Green #228 (B), and 1 ball in Scarlet #255 (C), or yarn that will k to the gauge given below

Size 6 (4mm) knitting needles or size needed to match gauge given below

Size 3 (3.25mm) knitting needles

Tapestry needle, stitch holders

Hat

1 (1, 2) ball A, 1 ball each B and C
Crochet hook for top loops

Set (for three smallest sizes only)

2 (3, 4) balls A, 1 (2, 2) ball B, and 1 (2, 2) ball C

∴ SIZES

6–9 months (1–2, 3–4, 5–6, 7–8, 9–10 years)
Length: 10¾ (12, 13¼, 14¼, 15½, 16¾) in.
Chest: 21½ (25, 28½, 31, 33½, 35½) in.
Hat circumference: S-16 (M-18, L-19½) in.

∴ GAUGE

20 sts and 28 rows to 4 in./10cm over st st on size
6 needles
Don't waste precious time and precious yarn—make
a gauge swatch before beginning!

∴ STITCH PATTERN

Stripe pattern (in st st): eight rows A, three rows B

VEST

Back

With size 3 needles and C, CO 54 (62, 70, 78, 84,
88) sts. Work in k2, p2 rib for ¾ in., ending with a
WS row. Change to size 6 needles and A. Begin
stripe pattern, working 8 rows A, then 3 rows B.
Cont working with patt as established until back
measures 6¼ (6¾, 7¼, 7¾, 8¼, 8¾) in., ending with
a WS row.

Shape armhole: BO 4 sts beg next 2 rows. Then
dec 1 st each end every RS row 6 times to 34 (42,
50, 58, 64, 68) sts. Cont without further shaping
until armhole measures 4½ (5¼, 6, 6½, 7¼, 8) in.

Shape shoulders: BO 4 (5, 7, 8, 9, 9) sts beg next
2 rows. Then BO 3 (5, 6, 7, 8, 9) sts beg next
2 rows. Put remaining 20 (22, 24, 28, 30, 32) sts
onto holder for neck to be worked later.

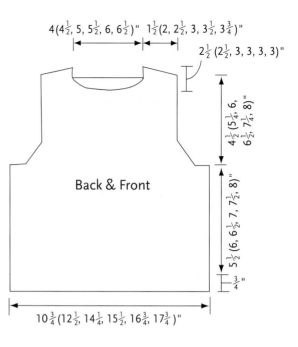

4(4½, 5, 5½, 6, 6½)" 1½(2, 2½, 3, 3½, 3¾)"

2½ (2½, 3, 3, 3, 3)"

4½ (5¼, 6, 6½, 7¼, 8)"

5½ (6, 6½, 7, 7½, 8)"

¾"

Back & Front

10¾ (12½, 14¼, 15½, 16¾, 17¾)"

CHAIN STITCH

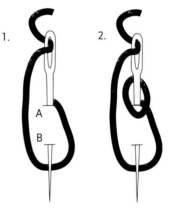

1. 2.

A

B

Step 1: Bring needle up at A. Re-insert at A, and
come out at B, drawing needle over loop of yarn
as shown.

Step 2: Re-insert needle at B and rep.

Front

Work as for back until armhole measures 2 (2¾, 3, 3½, 4¼, 5) in., ending with a RS row.

Shape right neck and shoulder: Work first 14 (17, 20, 22, 24, 25) sts, turn, and leave rem sts on holder for later. Working right shoulder sts only and maintaining stripe patt, dec 1 st at neck edge next 4 rows, and then 1 st at neck edge every other row 3 times to 7 (10, 13, 15, 17, 18) sts. Work until armhole measures 4¼ (5, 5¾, 6¼, 7, 7¾) in., ending with a RS row.

Next row: BO first 4 (5, 7, 8, 9, 9) sts, work to end.

Next row: Work even.

Next row: BO rem 3 (5, 6, 7, 8, 9) sts.

Shape left neck and shoulder: Slip the center 6 (8, 10, 14, 16, 18) sts onto holder for later. Then slip the rem 14 (17, 20, 22, 24, 25) sts onto a needle. Beg with a RS row, rejoin yarn, and work 1 row even. Shape neck as on right shoulder, and cont working until armhole measures 4¼ (5, 5¾, 6¼, 7, 7¾) in., ending with a WS row. Shape and BO shoulder as on right shoulder.

Finishing

Weave in loose ends. Sew right shoulder seam.

Neckband: With RS facing, use size 3 needle and C to pick up and k 18 (18, 20, 20, 20, 20) sts down left front neck, k across the 6 (8, 10, 14, 16, 18) sts on holder for front neck, pick up and k 18 (18, 20, 20, 20, 20) sts up right front neck to shoulder seam, k across the 20 (22, 24, 28, 30, 32) sts on holder for back neck—62 (66, 74, 82, 86, 90) sts. Work in k2, p2 rib for ¾ in. BO in rib. Sew together left shoulder seam and neckband. Lightly steam seams and front and back, avoiding ribbing.

Armbands: With RS facing, use size 3 needle and C to pick up and k 27 (31, 35, 37, 41, 45) sts up left front armhole, and then same number of sts down left back armhole—54 (62, 70, 74, 82, 90) sts. Work in k2, p2 rib for ¾ in. BO in rib. Repeat for right armband, starting at back. Weave in loose ends. Sew side seams and lightly steam, avoiding ribbing.

HAT

With size 3 needles and C, CO 80 (88, 96) sts. Work in st st for 1½ in., ending with a WS row. Work in k2, p2 rib for ½ in., ending with a WS row. Change to larger needles and A. Work stripe patt (8 rows A, 3 rows B) for 2½ in., ending with a WS row.

Shape top as follows:

First dec row (RS): *K2tog, k 16 (18, 20), skp*; rep from * to * 3 more times.
Work 3 rows even.

Next dec row (RS): *K2tog, k 14 (16, 18), skp*; rep from * to * 3 more times.
Work 3 rows even.

Next dec row: *K2tog, k 12 (14, 16), skp*; rep from * to * 3 more times.
Cont decreasing 8 sts as set every fourth row until 40 (48, 56) sts remain. Then work decreases as set every RS row until 8 sts remain. P 1 row even.

Last row: *K2tog, skp*; rep from * to * one more time.
Cut yarn, leaving a long tail to sew back seam, bring end through rem 4 sts, and tighten.

Finishing

Weave in loose ends. Sew back seam, reversing and using C for rolled edge. With tapestry needle and C, embroider in chain st, as shown on p. 25, up each dec axis to top of hat.

Loops: Using a crochet hook and C, make three 4-in. chains, leaving tails at each end for sewing to top of hat. Sew to top, forming loops, and weave in ends.

HOODWINKED

My mother-in-law told me that her mother knit matching
hooded zip-up sweaters for my husband and his brother
when they were babies and that they wore them all of the
time. I thought that sounded like a good idea, so I came
up with this one. I've never been one to use zippers,
but sometimes they really are just the perfect thing—especially
if you're trying to get a squirming toddler dressed to go
outdoors. This jacket is knit in one piece for the body,
so there is minimal finishing, and not a lot of loose ends
to weave in. It has Fair Isle borders and cable detailing at
the shoulders and around the front edges, so it never gets
boring to work on. And if you've never sewn in a zipper,
don't worry. It's not at all hard.

HOOD-WINKED

Hooded Zipper Jacket and Mittens

❖ MATERIALS

Jacket

6 (6, 7, 8, 9) 50g balls Filatura di Crosa Primo (76½ yd. per ball) in blue #118 (A) and 2 (2, 2, 2, 3) balls in chartreuse #261 (B), or other chunky yarn that will knit to the gauge given below
Size 6 (4mm) circ needle, 29 in.
Size 8 (5mm) circ needle, 24 in. to 29 in.
Size 9 (5.5mm) circ needle, 24 in. to 29 in.
Three Size 8 (5mm) dpns for shoulder and hood seams
11 (12, 13, 14, 15) in. separating zipper and thread to match A
Cable needle, stitch markers, tapestry needle, stitch holders, row counter, pins

Mittens

1 ball each A and B
Sizes 6 and 8 dpns

Set

6 (6, 7, 8, 9) balls A, 2 (3, 3, 3, 3) balls B

❖ SIZES

6 months (1, 2, 3, 4 years)
Length: 11½ (12½, 13½, 14½, 15½) in.
Chest: 24 (26, 28, 30, 32) in.
Sleeve: 6½ (7½, 8½, 9½, 10½) in.
Mittens: 1–2 (3–4) years

❖ GAUGE

20 sts and 22 rows to 4 in./10cm in color patts on size 9 (5.5mm) needles
Generic gauge: 17 sts and 22 rows to 4 in. over st st on size 8 needles
Don't waste precious time and precious yarn—make a gauge swatch before beginning!

❖ STITCH PATTERN

Cable panel (over 8 sts)

Row 1 (RS): P1, k6, p1.

Row 2: K1, p6, k1.

Row 3: As for row 1.

Row 4: As for row 2.

Row 5: P1, slip next 3 sts onto cn, hold at front, k next 3 sts, k the 3 sts from cn, and p1.

Row 6: As for row 2.

JACKET

Body

With size 6 circ needle and B, CO 97 (105, 113, 121, 129) sts. Beg with a k row, work 5 rows st st.

Next row (WS): K this row for turning hem. Beg with a k row, work three rows st st. Change to A, and p one row. Change to size 9 needles.

Next row (RS): Using A and B and beg with row 1 where indicated on chart A, work 10 rows chart. Change to size 8 needles and B only, and work 3 rows st st. Change back to A only, and p 1 row.

Next row (RS)—inc for cable: K1, [k1, m1] 3 times, k across until 4 sts rem, [m1, k1] 3 times, end k1— 103 (111, 119, 127, 135) sts.

Next row (WS): P2, k1, p6, k1, p to last 10 sts, k1, p6, k1, p2.

Next row (RS)—establish cable: K2, work row 1 cable, k across to last 10 sts, work row 1 cable, k2.

Next row (WS): P2, work row 2 cable, p to last 10 sts, work row 2 cable, p2.

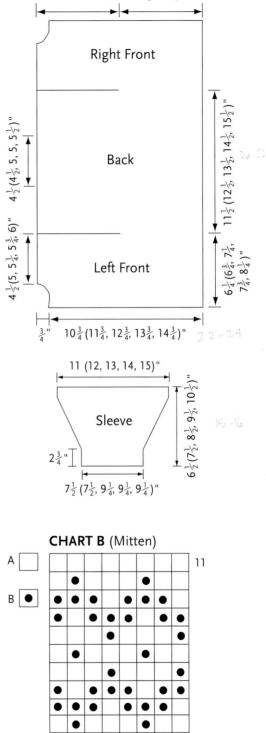

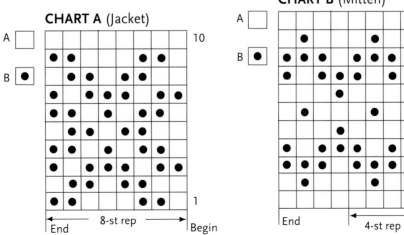

Back to right front section—still on RS, CO 9 additional sts to right needle for cable at armhole—36 (38, 40, 42, 44) sts.

Next row (WS): Work even, maintaining cable at end of row.

Next row (RS): Patt to last 9 sts; then establish cable at armhole by working same row of cable here as at beg of row, end k1.

Next row (WS): K1, work cable over next 8 sts, work across to last 10 sts, work cable over 8 sts, end p2.
Cont with patts as set, working cables at beginning and end, and ending each RS row and beginning each WS row with a k st.
Work until right front measures 10¾ (11¾, 12¾, 13¾, 14¾) in. from turning row, ending with a WS row.

Next row (RS)—shape neck: Patt across first 10 (10, 11, 11, 12) sts, and put on holder for later, work to end. (Make note of row number.)

Next row (WS): Work even.

Next row (RS): Ssk, work to end.

Next row (WS): Work even.

Next row (RS): Ssk, work to end—24 (26, 27, 29, 30) sts.
Work until piece measures 11½ (12½, 13½, 14½, 15½) in. from turning row, and put sts on holder. Leave a long tail for knitting shoulders tog later. (Make note of row number.)

Upper left front

Put the 27 (29, 31, 33, 35) sts from holder for left front onto needle so that you're ready to begin a RS row. CO 9 sts beg this row for cable at armhole, and work across to last 10 sts, picking up where you left off in cable patt.

Next row (WS): P2, work appropriate row of cable; p to end.

Next row (RS)—establish cable on new sts: K1, work same row of cable as at end of this row

Cont working with cable patts at each end as set until body measures 6 (6½, 7, 7½, 8) in. from turning row, ending with a WS row. (Make a note of row number.)

Upper right front

Next row (RS)—separate for armholes: Work across first 27 (29, 31, 33, 35) sts, maintaining cable and keeping track of row number, and put next 49 (53, 57, 61, 65) sts onto holder for back, then last 27 (29, 31, 33, 35) sts onto a second holder for left front for later.

over next 8 sts, k across to last 10 sts, work cable, end k2.

Cont working cables at each end as set, beg each RS row and ending each WS row with a k st, and work until left front measures 10¾ (11¾, 12¾, 13¾, 14¾) in., ending with a WS row.

Next row (RS)—shape neck: Work across until 10 (10, 11, 11, 12) sts rem. Put these rem sts onto holder for later, turn.

Next row (WS): Work even, maintaining cable patt at armhole.

Next row (RS): Work across to last 2 sts, k2tog.

Next row (WS): Work even.

Next row (RS): Work to last 2 sts, k2tog—24 (26, 27, 29, 30) sts.
Finish from here as for right front.

Upper back

Put rem center 49 (53, 57, 61, 65) sts onto needle so that you begin with a RS row.

First row: CO 9 sts beg row, work across these and center sts to end; CO another 9 sts this end onto right needle—67 (71, 75, 79, 83) sts total.

Next row (WS): P.

Next row (RS): K1, work same row of cable patt that you began with on CO sts for left and right fronts, k across to last 9 sts, work same row cable patt, end k1.

Cont on back with cables as set, working a k st at beg and end of every row. Work until back measures 11½ (12½, 13½, 14½, 15½) in. above turning row, ending with the same row as for fronts. Put first 24 (26, 27, 29, 30) sts onto holder for shoulder, put center 19 (19, 21, 21, 23) sts onto second holder for neck, and put rem 24 (26, 27, 29, 30) sts onto size 8 dpn. Put corresponding front shoulder sts onto second dpn. With a third dpn, knit shoulder seam tog as follows:

Hold the two needles with sts on them parallel with RSs facing each other. Insert a third dpn into the first st on the first needle as if to k, then into the first st on the second needle as if to k, and k the 2 sts as one. Rep this a second time—there should now be 2 sts on the right needle. *Pass the first st on the right needle over the second and BO.* K the next set of sts on the dpns tog, and rep from * to *. Cont in this way, knitting the corresponding sts of each shoulder tog and binding off as you go, until 1 st remains on the right needle. Break yarn, pull through last st to secure. Rep this process for other shoulder.

Sleeves

With size 6 needles and B, CO 33 (33, 41, 41, 41) sts. Beg with a k row, work 2 rows st st. *Change to A, and work 2 rows. Change to B, and work 2 rows.* Rep from * to * twice more.

Next row (RS): P this row in B for turning hem. Still in B, and beg with a p row, work two rows st st. Change to A, and p one row.

Next row (RS): Change to largest needles, and using yarns A and B, beg patt from chart A. Work 10 rows of chart.
Change to size 8 needles and B only, and work two rows st st. Change back to A only.

Next row (RS)—shape sleeve: Inc 1 st each end this row.
Then inc 1 st each end every RS row 5 (7, 0, 1, 2) times, then every fourth row 1 (1, 6, 7, 8) time to 47 (51, 55, 59, 63) sts.
Work until sleeve measures 6½ (7½, 8½, 9½, 10½) in. from turning row. BO, leaving a long tail to sew sleeve to armhole.

Hood

With RS facing, size 8 needles and A, and beg at right front neck edge, work across the first 10 (10, 11, 11, 12) sts from holder, maintaining cable patt where you left off, pick up and k 5 sts up right front neck shaping to shoulder seam. K across first 9 (9, 10, 10, 11) sts from holder for back neck, place marker, k1 (axis st), place marker. Work across rem 9 (9, 10, 10, 11) sts from holder, pick up and k 5 sts down left front neck shaping, work across 10 (10, 11, 11, 12) sts on holder, working cable where you left off—49 (49, 53, 53, 57) sts.

Work five rows in st st, maintaining cables at each edge, and slipping markers.

Next row (RS): Work to first marker, m1 (right slant—pick up loop by inserting needle from back to front under horizontal strand bet last st worked and next st on left needle, and k this loop through the front), slip first marker, k1 (axis st), slip second marker, m1 (left slant—pick up loop by inserting left needle from front to back under horizontal strand bet last st worked and next st on left needle, and k this through back of loop), work to end of row—51 (51, 55, 55, 59) sts. Cont as set, working increases as established on either side of axis st every RS row 3 (4, 3, 3, 3) times and then every fourth row 6 times to 69 (71, 73, 73, 77) sts. Cont without shaping until hood measures approx 8¾ (9¼, 9¾, 10¼, 10¾) in. from picked-up sts, ending with row 6 or row 1 of cable repeat.

Finishing hood: Put first 34 (35, 36, 36, 38) sts onto size 8 dpn. Put rem 35 (36, 37, 37, 39) sts onto another dpn. Hold the needles parallel with RSs facing each other—and beg at hood outer edge where cable is—k hood seam tog as for shoulders, working the last st alone. Pull yarn through st and secure.

Finishing

With 29-in. size 6 circ needle and A, start at turning ridge of lower right front and pick up and k 51 (56, 61, 65, 70) sts up 10¾ (11¾, 12¾, 13¾, 14¾) in. to neck shaping, then 83 (88, 93, 97, 103) sts around edge of hood to left front neck shaping, then 51 (56, 61, 65, 70) sts down left front to turning ridge—185 (200, 215, 227, 243) sts total. K 1 row, and then BO knitwise next row.

Weave in loose ends, except those needed for sewing seams. Lightly steam all parts to block, including all finished seams.

Center top of sleeves to shoulder seams with RSs facing each other; pin and backstitch in place. Sew inside sleeve seams. Steam seams.

Pin zipper to WS on each side of front so that only the teeth are exposed. Using matching thread, topstitch zipper along front edges from RS, and then turn and whipstitch outside edges of zipper to WS of inside fronts. Fold top edges of zipper back, and tack in place.

Fold all hems at turning rows, and pin in place. Sew hems with matching yarn. Steam hems.

Hood tassel: Cut a 3½-in. piece of cardboard. Take yarn B, and wrap around cardboard about 50 times. Cut end. With yarn still wrapped around cardboard, take another strand of B, threaded through a tapestry needle, and pull through the bottom edge bet cardboard and wrapped strands. Tie it tightly in a knot to secure bottom of tassel. Now insert scissors into the top edge bet the cardboard and wrapped strands, and cut to free the tassel from the cardboard. Cut another short length of B, and tie it around the strands about ¾ in. above the tail. Pull the ends of this piece into the strands of the tassel to hide them, and cut to same length as tassel strands. Use the tail to sew tassel to point of hood.

Zipper pull tassel: Follow instructions for hood tassel, only use a 2-in. piece of cardboard, and wrap 10 times. Thread tail ends through a tapestry needle, and then thread tapestry needle through hole in zipper pull. Pull tapestry needle down through center of tassel, tie ends in a knot hidden deep in tassel, and cut ends to same length as tassel ends to conceal.

MITTENS

Right mitten

With size 6 dpn and B, cast 28 (32) sts onto 3 dpns. Join rnd and p 2 rnds.
Change to A and B, and work 11 rnds from chart B.
Change to size 8 dpn and B only, and work st st (k every rnd) for 1 in.

Thumb opening: K first st from first needle, CO 5 (6) sts to right (working) needle using backward loops or finger CO method, slip next 5 (6) sts on first needle onto a holder for later, work to end of rnd.
Cont working until mitten body measures 2¾ (3¼) in. from end of color patt*. Now arrange sts on needles so that first 7 (8) sts are on first needle, next 7 (8) sts are on second needle, and rem 14 (16) sts are on third needle.

Shape top: Dec 1 st beg rnd by ssk; then k the last 2 sts of second needle tog; on third needle, beg by ssk, k across, then k last 2 sts tog. Rep this rnd until 8 sts rem total. Break yarn, pull through rem sts, and secure.

Thumb: With A and size 8 dpn, k across the 5 (6) sts from holder; then with a second and third dpn, pick up and k 7 (8) sts around rest of thumb opening—12 (14) sts total. Work in rnds for 1¼ (1¾) in.

Shape top of thumb: K2tog around, end k 0 (1)— 3 (4) sts rem. Break yarn, pull through rem sts, and tighten.

Finishing: Weave in loose ends. Pull ends from mitten top and thumb top to WS, and weave in.

Left mitten

Work as for right mitten to *. Arrange sts on needles so that first 7 (8) sts are on first needle, next 14 (16) sts are on second needle, and rem 7 (8) sts are on third needle.

Shape top: K across the sts on first needle until 2 sts rem, k2tog; on second needle, ssk, k to last 2 sts, k2tog; on third needle, ssk, k to end. Rep this dec rnd until 8 sts rem.
Finish from here, including thumb, as for the right mitten.

Mitten chain: Measure arm span of jacket wrist to wrist. Take a strand each of A and B that are double that length, and twist the two strands tog until quite firm. Then hold all four ends tog, and let the strands twist again by themselves to create a quadruple strand cord. Attach each end of cord to inside corner of mitten cuffs.

SWEDISH PANCAKES

I made this set so that I could use these
little pewter clasps. The front of the vest is worked
in a fairly simple two-color pattern, and the back is done
in an easy horizontal stripe. The stocking cap is actually
made up of two triangular pieces that are whipstitched
together in the accent color—a cinch to make.
I can't stand to weave in hundreds of loose ends at the end
of a project, so in this set, the two colors are carried up
the sides of the work. This vest is another one that can
be worn by a boy or a girl and that works nicely as
part of a colorful holiday outfit.

SWEDISH PANCAKES

Fair Isle Vest and Stocking Cap

Vest

1 (2, 2, 3, 3, 4, 4) 50g hank Classic Elite Tapestry (25% mohair, 75% wool, 95 yd. per hank) each in blue #2257 (A) and Daffodil #2296 (B) and 1 hank in Yak Black #2213 (C), or other worsted weight yarn that will k to gauge given below
Size 5 (3.75mm) knitting needles, or size needed to match gauge given below
Size 5 (3.75mm) circ knitting needle, 24 in. or 29 in.
Size 7 (4.5mm) knitting needles or size needed to match gauge given below
Three size 5 dpns for knitting shoulders together
Two stitch holders, row counter, tapestry needle, and markers
Three pewter clasps

Hat

1 hank each A, B, and C
Size 8 (5mm) knitting needles

Set

2 (2, 3, 4, 4, 5, 5) hanks each A and B and 1 hank C

:: SIZES

6 months (1–2, 3–4, 5–6, 7–8, 9–10, 11–12 years)
Chest at underarm: 20 (25, 27, 30, 32½, 36, 38½) in.
Length: 9 (10¾, 12½, 14, 15¾, 17½, 19) in.
Hat circumference: XS-16 (S-17, M-18½, L-19½) in.

:: GAUGE

Generic gauge (vest back): 22 sts and 28 rows to 4 in./10cm over st st on size 5 (3.75mm) needles
Generic gauge (hat): 18 sts and 24 rows to 4 in./10cm over st st on size 8 (5mm) needles
Fair Isle pattern gauge (vest fronts): 22 sts and 24 rows to 4 in./10cm on size 7 (4.5mm) needles
Don't waste precious time and precious yarn—make a gauge swatch before beginning!

❖ PATTERN STITCH

Stripe patt for vest (in st st)

Two rows A, two rows B. Don't cut yarn when changing colors—just carry the color not in use up the side of the work.

VEST

Back

With size 5 needle and A, CO 55 (69, 75, 82, 90, 99, 106) sts. Beg with a RS row, work 4-row stripe patt for 4½ (5½, 6½, 7½, 8½, 9½, 10½) in., ending with a WS row.

Shape armholes: BO 6 sts beg next 2 rows, then dec 1 st each end of every RS row (by ssk at beg of row, and k2tog at end of row) 3 (6, 5, 5, 5, 5, 5) times to 37 (45, 53, 60, 68, 77, 84) sts. Cont without further shaping until back measures 9 (10¾, 12½, 14, 15¾, 17½, 19) in. from beg, ending with a RS row (first row of new stripe).

Next row: P across first 8 (11, 14, 16, 19, 22, 24) sts for shoulder, BO center 21 (23, 25, 28, 30, 33, 36) sts for neck, and then p across rem 8 (11, 14, 16, 19, 22, 24) sts for second shoulder. Put both sets of shoulder sts onto holders, and set aside for later.

Left front

With size 7 needle and A, CO 13 (17, 19, 21, 25, 29, 33) sts.

First row (WS): P in A.

Second row (RS): Using A and B, beg color patt from chart where indicated for size being knit. After completing row 2 of chart, CO 3 (4, 4, 4, 4, 4, 4) sts beg next 3 (2, 2, 4, 4, 4, 4) RS rows, then 2 (3, 3, 0, 0, 0, 0) sts beg next 1 (2, 2, 0, 0, 0, 0) RS row, working new sts into color patt. At the same time, inc 1 st end of every RS row 3 (4, 4, 4, 4, 4, 4) times—27 (35, 37, 41, 45, 49, 53) sts. Place markers at beg and end of next row to use for measuring length, and cont from here in patt without further shaping until piece measures 4½ (5½, 6½, 7½, 8½, 9½, 10½) in. from markers, ending with a WS row.

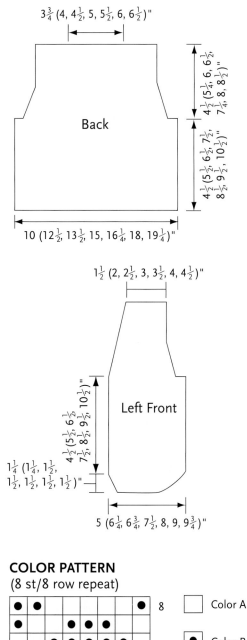

3¾ (4, 4½, 5, 5½, 6, 6½)"

Back

4½ (5¼, 6, 6½, 7¼, 8, 8½)"

4½ (5½, 6½, 7½, 8½, 9½, 10½)"

10 (12½, 13½, 15, 16¼, 18, 19¼)"

1½ (2, 2½, 3, 3½, 4, 4½)"

Left Front

4½ (5½, 6½, 7½, 8½, 9½, 10½)"

1¼ (1¼, 1½, 1½, 1½, 1½, 1½)"

5 (6¼, 6¾, 7½, 8, 9, 9¾)"

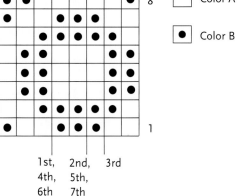

COLOR PATTERN
(8 st/8 row repeat)

8

1

1st, 4th, 6th

2nd, 5th, 7th

3rd

☐ Color A

● Color B

Shape armhole: BO 6 sts beg this RS row. Then shape rem armhole and neck simultaneously. Dec 1 st each end of every RS row—by ssk at beg of row, and k2tog at end of row—3 (6, 5, 5, 5, 5, 5) times, as you did for back, to 15 (17, 21, 25, 29, 33, 37) sts.

Cont neck shaping only by dec 1 st at end of every RS row 6 (5, 5, 6, 6, 6, 8) more times and then every fourth row 1 (1, 2, 3, 4, 5, 5) time to 8 (11, 14, 16, 19, 22, 24) sts.

Work without further shaping until front measures same as back. Cut yarn, leaving a long tail to k shoulder tog later, and leave sts on holder.

Right front

Beg and work as for left front through row 1 of chart. Then CO 3 (4, 4, 4, 4, 4) sts beg next 3 (2, 2, 4, 4, 4, 4) WS rows and then 2 (3, 3, 0, 0, 0, 0) sts beg next 1 (2, 2, 0, 0, 0, 0) WS row, working new sts into color patt. At the same time, inc 1 st end of every WS row 3 (4, 4, 4, 4, 4) times—27 (35, 37, 41, 45, 49, 53) sts.

Place markers at beg and end of next row to use for measuring. Work from here as for left front, only reverse armhole and neck shaping.

Finishing

Use the BO seam technique for shoulder seams as follows: With RSs facing each other, place the sts from the left front and back shoulder each onto a size 5 dpn, and hold the needles parallel. Insert a third dpn into the first st on the first needle as if to k, then into the first st on the second needle as if to k, and k the 2 sts as one. Rep this a second time—there should now be 2 sts on the right needle. *Pass the first st on the right needle over the second and BO*. K the next 2 sts on the parallel dpn tog, and rep from * to *. Cont in this way, knitting the corresponding sts of each shoulder tog and binding off as you go, until 1 st remains on the right needle. Break yarn, and pull through last st to secure. Rep this process for right shoulder.

Weave in loose ends. Lightly steam press pieces to block, including shoulder seams.

Armhole edging: With size 5 circ needle and C, starting at left front armhole edge with RS facing, pick up and k 27 (30, 34, 37, 41, 45, 48) sts up to shoulder seam and then same number of sts down other side to armhole edge—54 (60, 68, 74, 82, 90, 96) sts total. K 2 rows; BO Knitwise.

Rep for second armhole.

Right front and back neck edging: With size 5 circ needle and C, starting at lower right front side edge with RS facing, pick up and k 30 (33, 36, 37, 41, 45, 49) sts across lower edge, then 59 (66, 78, 86, 96, 105, 115) sts up center front to shoulder seam, then 25 (27, 29, 32, 33, 36, 39) sts around back neck to left shoulder seam. Stop picking up here—114 (126, 143, 155, 170, 186, 203) sts total. Work as for armhole edgings.

Left front and lower back edging: First backstitch left side seam tog. Then with size 5 circ needle and C, starting at left shoulder seam with RS facing, pick up and k 26 (30, 34, 37, 41, 45, 49) sts down front edge, then 30 (33, 36, 37, 41, 45, 49) sts around lower edge to side seam, then 54 (67, 73, 81, 88, 98, 104) sts across lower back—143 (166, 187, 204, 225, 248, 268) sts total. Work as for other edgings.

Backstitch rem side seam, including edging, and join edging at shoulder and underarms. Steam entire vest to block. Sew pewter clasps evenly spaced along straight part of front edges.

STOCKING CAP

Front half
With size 8 needles and C, CO 36 (38, 42, 44) sts. Work 12 rows st st for rolled brim.

Change to B, and beg stripe patt (6 rows B, 6 rows A, and carry yarn up side of work as for vest back). Work stripe patt for 3½ (4, 4½, 5) in., ending with a WS row.

Shape top: Dec 1 st at each end (by ssk beg row and k2tog end of row) this row and then every RS row until 4 sts rem. Break yarn, pull through sts, and secure.

Back half
Work as for front half.

Finishing
Weave in loose ends. Steam halves to block, omitting rolled brim. Using tapestry needle and yarn C, whip-stitch up sides with RSs out—it should look sort of crude and homespun. Sew brim seams on RS, and allow to roll.

Tassel:
Cut a 3½-in. piece of cardboard (about the size of a business card). Take yarn C, and wrap around cardboard about 50 times. Cut end. With yarn still wrapped around cardboard, take another strand of C, and pull through the bottom edge bet cardboard and wrapped strands. Tie it tightly in a knot to secure bottom of tassel. Now insert scissors into the top edge bet the cardboard and wrapped strands, and cut to free the tassel from the cardboard. Cut a short length of A, and tie it around the strands about ¾ in. above the tail. Pull the ends of this piece into the strands of the tassel to hide them, and cut to a shorter length than tassel strands. Use the tail to sew tassel to point of hat.

ELECTRIC SMOCK

For the little girl who has everything.
This smock coat and hat were very fun to
design and knit. The set has a few different not-so-difficult
color patterns to work, plus a ruffle, and then
a simple seed stitch pattern for most of the gathered
skirt and sleeves. I knit mine in cotton, but I have
always thought that it would work well in wool and
in more wintry colors. The button band spans only
the length of the bodice, but it could easily be
extended the entire length of the smock,
making it more of a coatdress.

ELECTRIC SMOCK

Ruffled Cotton Smock and Hat with Fair Isle Detailing

∴ **MATERIALS**

Smock

2 (2, 2, 3) 125g skeins Classic Elite Provence (100% cotton, 256 yd./233m per skein) in Clear Blue Sky #2607 (A) and 1 skein each in Peony Pink #2630 (B) and Helianthus Gold #2696 (C), or yarn that will knit to the gauge given below
Three ½-in. buttons
Size 6 (4mm) knitting needles, or size needed to match gauge given below
Set of size 6 dpns
Tapestry needle and stitch holders

Hat

1 skein each A, B, and C
Set of size 3 (3.25mm) dpns for I-cord bow

Set

2 (3, 3, 3) skeins A, 1 skein each B and C

∴ **SIZES**

6–9 months (1, 2, 3 years)
Length: 11 (12½, 14, 15¼) in.
Chest: 20 (22, 24, 26) in.
Sleeve: 7 (7½, 8½, 9½) in.
Hat circumference: 15½ (16¾, 17½, 18¾) in.

∴ **GAUGE**

22 sts and 27 rows to 4 in./10cm over simple seed st on size 6 needle
24 sts and 27 rows to 4 in./10cm over color patts on size 6 needle
Don't waste precious time and precious yarn—make a gauge swatch before beginning!

∴ **PATTERN STITCH**

Simple seed st (multiple of 4 sts)

> **Row 1:** [K3, p1] to end.
>
> **Rows 2 and 4:** P.
>
> **Rows 3 and 7:** K.
>
> **Row 5:** K1, *p1, k3*; rep from * to * across row to last 3 sts, p1, k2.
>
> **Rows 6 and 8:** P.

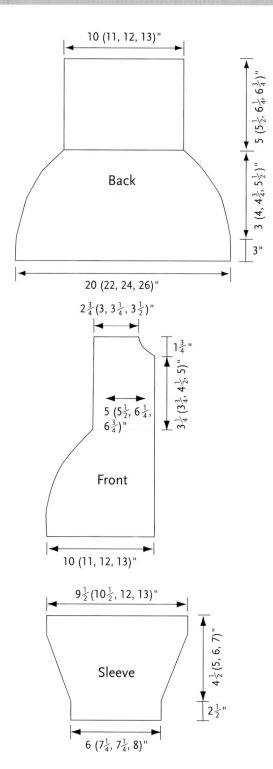

10 (11, 12, 13)"

Back

5 ($5\frac{1}{2}$, $6\frac{1}{4}$, $6\frac{3}{4}$)"

3 (4, $4\frac{3}{4}$, $5\frac{1}{2}$)"

3"

20 (22, 24, 26)"

$2\frac{3}{4}$ (3, $3\frac{1}{4}$, $3\frac{1}{2}$)"

$1\frac{3}{4}$"

5 ($5\frac{1}{2}$, $6\frac{1}{4}$, $6\frac{3}{4}$)"

$3\frac{1}{4}$ ($3\frac{3}{4}$, $4\frac{1}{2}$, 5)"

Front

10 (11, 12, 13)"

$9\frac{1}{2}$ ($10\frac{1}{2}$, 12, 13)"

$4\frac{1}{2}$ (5, 6, 7)"

Sleeve

$2\frac{1}{2}$"

6 ($7\frac{1}{4}$, $7\frac{1}{4}$, 8)"

CHART A (12-st rep)

A **+**

B **●**

C ☐

11

5

6 mo, 2 yr.
& right front

1 yr. & 3 yr.

CHART B (6-st rep)

1 yr. & 3 yr.

6 mo, 2 yr.
& right front

CHART C (4-st rep)

7

Beg here
for all sizes

SMOCK

Back

With size 6 needle and B, CO 121 (132, 143, 154) sts.
Break yarn, and change to A. Work scallop ruffle
as follows:

Row 1 (RS): K.

Row 2: P.

Row 3: *[P2tog] 2 times, [m1, k1] 3 times, m1,
[p2tog] 2 times*; rep from * to * to end.

Row 4: P.

Rows 5 and 6: K.

Row 7: K all sts, increasing o (1, 2, 3) sts evenly across to 121 (133, 145, 157) sts.

Next row (WS): Change to C, and p this row.

Next row: Beg chart patt A, starting rep where indicated on chart for the size you're knitting, and work across to end.
Cont chart patt through last row.

Next row (WS): P this row in C only, decreasing 1 st to 120 (132, 144, 156) sts.
Break yarn, change to A, and work 2 rows st st.

Next row (RS): Work row one of simple seed st patt.
Cont working patt for 3 (4, 4¾, 5½) in., ending with a WS row.

Next row: K1, *k2tog; rep from * to last st, end k1—61 (67, 73, 79) sts. P 1 row.

Next row (RS): Change to yarns B and C, and work from chart patt B, beg where indicated on chart for the size you're knitting.
Work patt as set for 5 (5½, 6¼, 6¾) in., ending with a WS row.

Next row: Patt 17 (18, 20, 21) sts and put onto a holder, BO center 27 (31, 33, 37) sts, patt rem 17 (18, 20, 21) sts, and put on holder for later.

Right front
With size 6 needle and B, CO 59 (66, 70, 77) sts. Change to A, and work scallop ruffle as follows.

Row 1: K.

Row 2: P.

Row 3 (6-month and 2-year sizes only): *[P2tog] 4 times, [m1, k1] 3 times, m1*. Rep from * to * across to last 4 sts, [p2tog] twice—ending with 57 (6 months) and 68 (2 years) sts.

Ruffle row 3 (1- and 3-year sizes only): *[P2tog] twice, [m1, k1] three times, m1, [p2tog] twice*. Rep from * to * to end of row.

All sizes—row 4: P.

Rows 5 and 6: K.

Row 7: K, increasing 4 (1, 5, 2) sts evenly across to 61 (67, 73, 79) sts.

Next row (WS): Change to C, and p one row.

Next row (RS): Beg row one of chart A where indicated for size you're knitting, and cont through last row of chart.

Next row: P this row in C only, decreasing 1 st to 60 (66, 72, 78) sts.

Next row: Change to A, work 2 rows st st.

Next row (RS): Starting with row one, beg simple seed st, and work for 3 (4, 4¾, 5½) in., ending with a WS row.

Next row: K1, *k2tog; rep from *, end k1—31 (34, 37, 40) sts. P 1 row. Break yarn, change to B and C, and work from chart B, beg where indicated for the size you're knitting. Work patt for 3¼ (3¾, 4½, 5) in., ending with a WS row.

Shape neck: Maintaining patt, BO 6 (7, 7, 8) sts beg next row. Work 1 row even. BO 3 (4, 5, 6) sts beg next row. Then dec 1 st at neck edge on every row 5 times to 17 (18, 20, 21) sts. Work until front measures same as back.
Put sts onto holder for later.

Left front
Work as for right front through first two rows.

Row 3: *[P2tog] twice, [m1, k1] three times, m1, [p2tog] twice*. Rep from * to * to end for 1-year and 3-year sizes and to last 4 sts for 6-month and 2-year sizes, ending [p2tog] twice. Work as for right front from here on, only beg charts A and B where indicated for size you're knitting, and

reverse neck shaping by starting with WS row. Put shoulder sts onto holder for later.

Sleeves
With size 6 needles and B, CO 33 (44, 44, 44) sts. Change to A, and work scallop ruffle as for back, through row 6.

Row 7: K all sts, increasing 4 (1, 1, 5) sts evenly across to 37 (45, 45, 49) sts.

Next row (WS): Change to C, and p this row.

Next row: Work row one of chart C, beg where indicated on chart.
Complete all rows of chart.

Next row (WS): P this row in C only.
Change to A, and k one row.

Next row: P.

Next row (RS): Beg simple seed st, increasing 1 st each end this row.
Then inc 1 st each end every other row 1 (0, 3, 2) time, then every fourth row 6 (6, 7, 9) times to 53 (59, 67, 73) sts, working increases into st patt. Work even in patt until sleeve measures 4½ (5, 6, 7) in. from beg of simple seed st. BO sts.

Collar
Before working the collar, the shoulder seams should be ktog as follows: With RSs facing each other, place the sts from the left front and back shoulder each onto a size 6 dpn, and hold the two needles parallel to each other. Insert a third dpn into the first st on the first needle as if to k, then into the first st on the second needle as if to k, and k the 2 sts as one. Rep this a second time—there should now be 2 sts on the right needle. *Pass the first st on the right needle over the second and BO.* K the next set of sts on the parallel dpns together, and rep from * to *. Cont in this way, knitting the corresponding sts of each shoulder tog and binding off as you go, until 1 st remains on the right needle. Break yarn, pull through last st to secure.

Now beg collar: With size 6 needle and A, beg at left neck edge with WS facing, pick up and

k 17 (19, 20, 22) sts up neck shaping to shoulder seam, pick up and k 25 (28, 30, 33) sts across back neck, pick up and k 17 (19, 20, 22) sts down right neck to edge—59 (66, 70, 77) sts. Beg with a p row, work 1½ in. st st, ending with a WS row.

Next row: K2 into each st across to 118 (132, 140, 154) sts.

Next row: K1, p1 across.

Next row: P1, k1 across. Rep last 2 rows until collar measures 2¼ (2½, 2½, 2¾) in., ending with a RS row. BO in patt.

Finishing

Weave in loose ends.

Button band (left front): Starting at left front neck edge with RS facing, use size 6 needle and A to pick up and k 18 (20, 24, 26) sts down to where yoke color patt ends.

Row 1: P1, k1 across.

Row 2: K1, p1 across. Rep these two rows two more times. BO in patt.

Buttonhole band (right front): Starting at beg color patt for yoke on right front with RS facing, use size 6 needle and A to pick up and k 18 (20, 24, 26) sts up to neck edge.

Row 1: P1, k1 across.

Row 2: K1, p1 across.

Row 3: As for row one.

Row 4 (RS—buttonhole row): K1, k2tog, yo, k5 (6, 8, 9), k2tog, yo, k4 (5, 7, 8), k2tog, yo, k2.

Row 5: P.

Row 6: As for row two.

Row 7: BO in [p1, k1]. Sew side and sleeve seams, matching up patts. Sew buttons opposite button-holes. Lightly steam garment.

HAT

With size 6 needle and B, CO 187 (198, 209, 220) sts. Change to A, and work scallop ruffle as follows.

Row 1: K.

Row 2 (WS): P.

Row 3: *[P2tog] twice, [m1, k1] three times, m1, [p2tog] twice*; rep from * to * to end.

Row 4: P.

Row 5: K1 (2, 1, 3), *k2tog; rep from *, end k0 (2, 0, 3)—93 (101, 105, 113) sts.

Row 6: K.

Row 7: Change to C, and p this row.

Next row (RS): Beg chart C where indicated for size you're knitting.
Complete all rows of chart. P one more row in C only. Change to A, and k one row.

Next row: P to last 2 sts, m1, p2—94 (102, 106, 114) sts. (This last inc will line up seed st patt with color patt.)

Next row (RS): Work row one of simple seed st, ending with k2.

Rows 2 and 4: P.

Row 3: K.

Row 5: Work row five of simple seed st, ending with p1.

Rows 6 and 8: P.

Row 7: K. Cont with patt as set until piece measures approx 4 (4½, 5, 5½) in. from end of Fair Isle patt, ending with row two or six of simple seed st patt.

Shape crown: K2tog across to 47 (51, 53, 57) sts.

Next row: P2tog across, until 3 sts rem, end p3tog—23 (25, 26, 28) sts.

Next row: K2tog across, end k1 (1, 0, 0)—12 (13, 13, 14) sts.

Work I-cord bow: Break yarn, leaving a long enough tail to sew back seam. Put first 6 (6, 6, 7) sts onto a holder. Put rem 6 (7, 7, 7) sts onto a size 3 dpn. Joining yarn B and starting with a RS row, work I-cord as follows: K across row with a second dpn. *Slide the sts to the opposite end of the needle, and k them.* Rep from * to * for 3½ in. Break yarn, and pull through sts and tighten. Put sts from holder onto the dpn, and work as for first half of bow.

Finishing

Weave in loose ends. Thread I-cord ends into a tapestry needle, and bring the tails down through the center of I-cords to conceal and secure. Tie the two I-cords into a double knot. Sew back seam. With a little bit of yarn C threaded into a tapestry needle, tack I-cord bow to keep it from coming undone.

PREMATURELY GRAY

This jacket looks double-breasted, but it's not.
One front is about one-third the entire width of the sweater
and the other about two-thirds. It knits up in no time
and is very warm—perfect for a late fall everyday jacket.
This one in particular has a broad size range: It goes from
6 months to a woman's large. And although it is decidedly
feminine as an adult sweater, it looks fine on a baby
or toddler boy. When I was working out the initial design
and experimenting with various stitch patterns, I found
that the broken rib looked so good on both sides that I couldn't
decide at first which to call the right side. Obviously I went
with the smoother rib pattern for the right side, but you can
see the bumpy stitch peeking out on the rolled-up sleeve.

PREMATURELY GRAY

Rib-Stitch Side-Buttoning Jacket with Hat

⋮ MATERIALS

Jacket
3 (4, 5, 5, 6, 7, 8, 9, 11) 100g skeins Brown Sheep Lamb's Pride Superwash Bulky (100% wool, 110 yd./101m per skein) in Charcoal Heather #SW04 (MC), and 1 (1, 1, 1, 1, 2, 2, 2, 2) skein in Shane's Red #SW84 (CC), or bulky yarn that will knit to the gauge given below
One ¾-in. button to match MC for under collar
Size 10½ (6.5mm) knitting needles, or size needed to match gauge given below
Size 10½ circ needle for picking up collar sts
Three size 10½ dpns for working shoulder seams
Two size 8 (5mm) dpns for making knit buttons
Size J or K crochet hook for trim
Tapestry needle, stitch holders, markers

Hat
1 skein each MC and CC
Size 9 (5.5mm) knitting needles for brim

Set
4 (4, 5, 6, 7, 8, 9, 10, 12) skeins MC, 2 skeins CC

⋮ SIZES
6–9 months (1–2, 3–4, 5–6, 7–8, 9–10, 11–12 years, women's S, women's L)
Length: 11½ (13, 15, 16½, 18, 19½, 21, 23, 24½) in.
Chest: 20 (24, 26, 29½, 32, 34, 36, 41, 45) in.
Sleeve: 9 (10, 11, 12, 13, 14, 15, 16, 18) in.
Hat circumference: S-15½ (M-17, L-18½, XL-20) in.

⋮ GAUGE
15 sts and 18 rows to 4 in./10cm in rib st on size 10½ needles
Generic gauge: 3¼ sts/in. in st st on size 10½ needles
Don't waste precious time and precious yarn—make a gauge swatch before beginning!

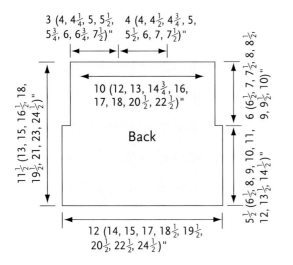

3 (4, 4$\frac{1}{4}$, 5, 5$\frac{1}{2}$, 5$\frac{3}{4}$, 6, 6$\frac{3}{4}$, 7$\frac{1}{2}$)"   4 (4, 4$\frac{1}{2}$, 4$\frac{3}{4}$, 5, 5$\frac{1}{2}$, 6, 7, 7$\frac{1}{2}$)"

10 (12, 13, 14$\frac{3}{4}$, 16, 17, 18, 20$\frac{1}{2}$, 22$\frac{1}{2}$)"

Back

11$\frac{1}{2}$ (13, 15, 16$\frac{1}{2}$, 18, 19$\frac{1}{2}$, 21, 23, 24$\frac{1}{2}$)"

6 (6$\frac{1}{2}$, 7, 7$\frac{1}{2}$, 8, 8$\frac{1}{2}$, 9, 9$\frac{1}{2}$, 10)"

5$\frac{1}{2}$ (6$\frac{1}{2}$, 8, 9, 10, 11, 12, 13$\frac{1}{2}$, 14$\frac{1}{2}$)"

12 (14, 15, 17, 18$\frac{1}{2}$, 19$\frac{1}{2}$, 20$\frac{1}{2}$, 22$\frac{1}{2}$, 24$\frac{1}{2}$)"

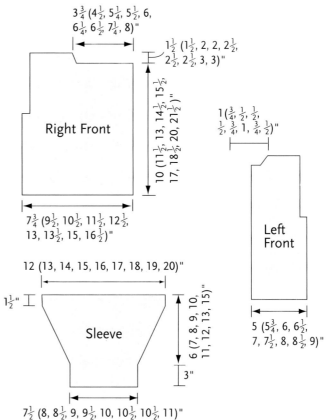

3$\frac{3}{4}$ (4$\frac{1}{2}$, 5$\frac{1}{4}$, 5$\frac{1}{2}$, 6, 6$\frac{1}{4}$, 6$\frac{1}{2}$, 7$\frac{1}{4}$, 8)"

1$\frac{1}{2}$ (1$\frac{1}{2}$, 2, 2, 2$\frac{1}{2}$, 2$\frac{1}{2}$, 2$\frac{1}{2}$, 3, 3)"

Right Front

10 (11$\frac{1}{2}$, 13, 14$\frac{1}{2}$, 15$\frac{1}{2}$, 17, 18$\frac{1}{2}$, 20, 21$\frac{1}{2}$)"

7$\frac{3}{4}$ (9$\frac{1}{2}$, 10$\frac{1}{2}$, 11$\frac{1}{2}$, 12$\frac{1}{2}$, 13, 13$\frac{1}{2}$, 15, 16$\frac{1}{2}$)"

1 ($\frac{3}{4}$, $\frac{1}{2}$, $\frac{1}{2}$, $\frac{1}{2}$, $\frac{3}{4}$, 1, $\frac{3}{4}$, $\frac{1}{2}$)"

Left Front

5 (5$\frac{3}{4}$, 6, 6$\frac{1}{2}$, 7, 7$\frac{1}{2}$, 8, 8$\frac{1}{2}$, 9)"

12 (13, 14, 15, 16, 17, 18, 19, 20)"

1$\frac{1}{2}$"

Sleeve

6 (7, 8, 9, 10, 11, 12, 13, 15)"

3"

7$\frac{1}{2}$ (8, 8$\frac{1}{2}$, 9, 9$\frac{1}{2}$, 10, 10$\frac{1}{2}$, 10$\frac{1}{2}$, 11)"

∴ PATTERN STITCH

Broken rib st

Row 1 (RS): K.

Row 2 (WS—for an odd number of sts): K1, *p1, k1; rep from * to end.

Row 2 (WS—for an even number of sts): K1, p1 across.

All pieces are worked entirely in rib st.

JACKET

Back

Using size 10$\frac{1}{2}$ needles and MC, CO 45 (53, 57, 63, 69, 73, 77, 84, 92) sts. Work in rib patt for 5$\frac{1}{2}$ (6$\frac{1}{2}$, 8, 9, 10, 11, 12, 13$\frac{1}{2}$, 14$\frac{1}{2}$) in.

BO 4 sts beg next 2 rows for armholes—37 (45, 49, 55, 61, 65, 69, 76, 84) sts.

Cont in patt until armhole measures 6 (6$\frac{1}{2}$, 7, 7$\frac{1}{2}$, 8, 8$\frac{1}{2}$, 9, 9$\frac{1}{2}$, 10) in. and back measures 11$\frac{1}{2}$ (13, 15, 16$\frac{1}{2}$, 18, 19$\frac{1}{2}$, 21, 23, 24$\frac{1}{2}$) in. total from beg. Put first 11 (15, 16, 19, 21, 22, 23, 25, 28) sts for one shoulder on holder, put center 15 (15, 17, 17, 19, 21, 23, 26, 28) sts onto holder for neck, and put remaining 11 (15, 16, 19, 21, 22, 23, 25, 28) sts onto holder for second shoulder.

Left front

Using size 10$\frac{1}{2}$ needles and MC, CO 19 (22, 23, 26, 28, 29, 31, 32, 35) sts. Work in rib patt for 5$\frac{1}{2}$ (6$\frac{1}{2}$, 8, 9, 10, 11, 12, 13$\frac{1}{2}$, 14$\frac{1}{2}$) in., ending with a WS row.

BO 4 sts beg next row for armhole—15 (18, 19, 22, 24, 25, 27, 28, 31) sts. Cont in patt until piece measures 10 (11$\frac{1}{2}$, 13, 14$\frac{1}{2}$, 15$\frac{1}{2}$, 17, 18$\frac{1}{2}$, 20, 21$\frac{1}{2}$) in. from beg, ending with a RS row.

Shape neck: BO 2 (1, 1, 1, 1, 1, 2, 1, 1) sts beg next row (neck edge); then dec 1 st beg every WS row 2 more times—11 (15, 16, 19, 21, 22, 23, 25, 28) sts. Work until piece measures same as back, and put sts onto holder for later, leaving a 20-in. tail for knitting shoulder tog later. Place first marker for buttons $\frac{3}{4}$ in. down from neck edge, place second marker 1 in. up from hemline, and place 3 (3, 3, 3, 3, 3, 3, 5, 5) more markers evenly spaced bet the top and bottom markers.

Sleeves

Using size 10½ needles and MC, CO 28 (30, 32, 34, 36, 38, 40, 40, 41) sts. Work in rib patt for 3 in., ending with a WS row.

Shape sleeve: Inc 1 st each end next row, maintaining patt, then every RS row 5 (5, 4, 4, 4, 4, 3, 7, 4) times, then every fourth row 2 (3, 5, 6, 7, 8, 10, 8, 12) times to 44 (48, 52, 56, 60, 64, 68, 72, 75) sts. Work patt without further shaping until sleeve measures 9 (10, 11, 12, 13, 14, 15, 16, 18) in. BO, leaving a tail double the measurement of the width of the top of the sleeve for sewing later.

Collar

Before working the collar, the shoulders need to be joined. Use the BO seam technique for shoulder seams as follows: With RSs facing each other, place the sts from the left front and back shoulder each onto a size 10½ dpn, and hold the needles parallel. Insert a third dpn into the first st on the first needle as if to k, then into the first st on the second needle as if to k, and k the 2 sts as one. Rep this a second time—there should now be 2 sts on the right needle. *Pass the first st on the right needle over the second and BO*. K the next 2 sts on the parallel dpns tog, and rep from * to *. Cont in this way, knitting the corresponding sts of each shoulder tog and binding off as you go, until 1 st remains on the right needle. Break yarn, pull through last st to secure. Rep this process for right shoulder. Weave in ends, except those you will be using for sewing. Lightly steam shoulder seams and all pieces to block.

Now you are ready to work the collar. Beg at left front neck with WS facing, size 10½-circ needle and CC, pick up and k 7 (7, 7, 7, 8, 9, 9, 10, 10) sts up left front neck, work across the 15 (15, 17, 17, 19, 21, 23, 26, 28) sts from holder for back neck, and then pick up and k 17 (20, 21, 23, 25, 26, 26, 30, 33) sts down right front neck to edge—39 (42, 45, 47, 52, 56, 58, 66, 71) sts. Beg with a WS row, work rib patt, and inc 1 st each end every RS row as follows: K1, m1, k across until 1 st remains, m1, k1. Work until collar measures 4 (4, 4½, 4½, 4½, 5, 5, 5, 5) in. from beg, ending with a RS row. BO loosely in patt.

Right front

Using size 10½ needles and MC, CO 29 (35, 39, 43, 47, 49, 51, 56, 62) sts. Work in rib patt, making buttonholes on RS rows opposite markers as you go as follows: K 4, BO 2 sts, work to end.

Next row: Work to bound-off sts, turn, CO 2, turn, and work rem 4 sts. At the same time, work until piece measures 5½ (6½, 8, 9, 10, 11, 12, 13½, 14½) in., ending with a RS row.
BO 4 sts for armhole beg next row—25 (31, 35, 39, 43, 45, 47, 52, 58) sts. Cont as set until piece measures 10 (11½, 13, 14½, 15½, 17, 18½, 20, 21½) in. from beg, ending with a WS row.

Shape neck: BO 12 (14, 17, 18, 20, 21, 22, 25, 28) sts beg next row (neck edge); then dec 1 st beg every RS row 2 more times—11 (15, 16, 19, 21, 22, 23, 25, 28) sts. Work until piece measures same as back. Put sts onto holder, and leave a 20-in. tail for knitting shoulder tog later.

Finishing

Gently steam collar.

Attach sleeves: Center sleeve on armhole with RSs facing each other, and pin in place. Backstitch sleeve top to armhole edge, sewing the bound-off stitches at armhole edges to the straight side edge at top of sleeve. Sew sleeve and side seams. Lightly press seams.

Trim: Starting at left front neck edge, use the crochet hook and CC to sc perimeter of jacket within ½ in. of right front neck edge. Chain st five for button loop, reattach where you left off, and sc to neck edge (for a neater look, crochet a little further to underneath collar). Cut yarn, and pull through last st. Work sc around cuffs. Sc in CC around outside of collar—this will give it a nice rounded shape. Weave in loose ends, and steam crocheted areas. Make 5 (5, 5, 5, 5, 5, 7, 7) buttons as described at right. Sew buttons opposite buttonholes, and sew the smaller regular button under collar opposite loop.

HAT

Start by making the brim in two separate flaps.

Small flap: With size 9 needle and CC, CO 18 (20, 22, 24) sts. Work in broken rib patt, increasing 1 st beg every RS row 5 times to 23 (25, 27, 29) sts. Work without further shaping until flap measures 3 in., ending with a RS row. Sl sts onto holder.

Large flap: With size 9 needle and CC, CO 30 (34, 38, 42) sts. Work in broken rib patt, increasing 1 st at the end of every RS row, maintaining patt, 5 times to 35 (39, 43, 47) sts. Cont without further shaping until piece measures 3 in., ending with a RS row. Leave sts on needle. Sl small flap sts onto the same needle so shaped ends face each other at center, with WS facing—58 (64, 70, 76) sts.

Body: Beg with this WS row, work in broken rib patt, still in CC, joining flaps. Cont in patt for 1 in., ending with a RS row. Change to size 10½ needles and MC, and beg with a RS row (WS now becomes RS), work broken rib for 4½ (5½, 6½, 8) in., ending with a RS row.

Knit Buttons

With size 8 dpn and CC, CO 3 sts, leaving a 10-in. tail at beg of CO edge (for sewing button to coat later). These buttons are worked in a manner similar to I-cord, but you will be shaping your tube by increasing and decreasing. To work I-cord, beg every row by sliding the sts to the opposite end of the needle, thereby pulling the working yarn from the bottom of the row to join.

Rows 1 and 2: K.
Row 3: K1, m1, k1, m1, k1—5 sts.
Rows 4 and 5: K.
Row 6: K2, m1, k1, m1, k2—7 sts.
Rows 7 and 8: K.
Row 9: K1, m1, k5, m1, k1—9 sts.
Row 10: K.
Row 11: Ssk, ssk, k1, k2tog, k2tog—5 sts.
Row 12: K.

Before continuing, take 1½ yd. of CC, and stuff it into the center of the tube, using the crochet hook to tamp it down.

Row 13: K.
Row 14: Ssk, k1, k2tog—3 sts.

Cut yarn, leaving a 10-in. tail. Pull through sts, and tighten. The button should look like an almond with pointy ends. Using the 10-in. tails, pull the ends tog toward the back (where you can see the join), and tie tog very tightly in a square knot, thereby forming the button into a ball about the size of a crabapple. Use ends to sew button to coat.

Next row: P2tog across—29 (32, 35, 38) sts.

Next row: K2tog across, end k 1 (0, 1, 0)—15 (16, 18, 19) sts. Break yarn, leaving a tail to sew back seam, pull through rem sts, and secure. Sew back seam to end of MC; then using CC, sew brim seam on reverse side. Weave in ends.

Finishing: With crochet hook and CC, beg at back seam and sc hem of brim on RS for a neat edge. Fold back brim. Make three k buttons in CC, as described in inset box, leaving 10-in. tails. Use these tails to sew buttons in a cluster to the top of the hat.

AQUA VELVET

When a friend of mine had a baby,
I knit a sage green chenille sweater like this one,
but without cables. I had wanted to make a matching hat,
but I found that the chenille didn't have enough elasticity
to hold onto a wiggly child's head. Instead I made
a black and white cotton striped stocking cap with
a matching green chenille tassel. That was the prototype.
For this set, I changed the color, added cables,
and changed the shape of the hat. My sister
said this yarn was like spun velvet,
so I called it Aqua Velvet.

AQUA VELVET

Chenille Double-Breasted Cabled Cardigan and Matching Cotton Striped Hat

∴ **MATERIALS**

Jacket
4 (5, 5, 6, 7) 50g skeins Crystal Palace Cotton Chenille (100% cotton, 98 yd./89m per skein) in turquoise #9687, or yarn that will knit to the gauge given below
Six ⅞-in. to 1-in. buttons
Size 6 (4mm) knitting needles
Size 7 (4.5mm) knitting needles, or size needed to match chenille gauge given below
Set of size 7 (4.5mm) dpns
Cable needle, tapestry needle, and stitch holders

Hat
1 skein each Tahki Cotton Classic (108 yd./98m per skein) in black (A) and natural white (B), or yarn that will knit to the cotton gauge given below
Leftover chenille for stitching and tassels
Size 6 (4mm) knitting needles, or size needed to match cotton gauge given below

∴ **SIZES**

3 months (6 months, 12–18 months, 2 years, 3 years)
Length: 8½ (10¼, 12¼, 14, 14) in.
Chest: 23 (24½, 26½, 28, 30) in.
Sleeve: 8 (8½, 9, 10, 11) in. (cuff will be turned up 1 in.)
Hat circumference: S-15½ (M-17, L-18½) in.

∴ **GAUGE**

Chenille: 16 sts and 24 rows to 4 in./10cm over st st on size 7 needle
Cotton: 22 sts and 28 rows to 4 in./10cm over st st on size 6 needles
Don't waste precious time and precious yarn—make a gauge swatch before beginning!

∴ **PATTERN STITCHES**

RSS: Reverse st st (p on RS, k on WS)
T3f: Slip next 2 sts onto cable needle, and hold at front of work; p1, and then k2 from cable needle
T3b: Slip next st onto cable needle, and hold at back of work; k2, and then p1 from cable needle.

Cable panel (17 sts)

Row 1 (WS): K6, p2, k1, p2, k6.

Row 2 (RS): P6, sl 3 sts to cn, and leave at front; k2, sl first st from cn back onto left needle, and p it; k2 from cn, p6.

Row 3: K6, p2, k1, p2, k6.

Row 4: P5, t3b, p1, t3f, p5.

Row 5: K5, p2, k3, p2, k5.

Row 6: P4, t3b, p3, t3f, p4.

Row 7: K4, p2, k2, k5 into next st by knitting into front, back, front, back, and front of st; k2, p2, k4.

Row 8: P3, t3b, p2, k5 tog tbl, p2, t3f, p3.

Row 9: K3, p2, k7, p2, k3.

Row 10: P2, t3b, p7, t3f, p2.

Row 11: K2, p2, k2, k5 into next st; k3, k5 into next st, k2, p2, k2.

Row 12: P1, t3b, p2, k5 tog tbl; p3, k5 tog tbl; p2, t3f, p1.

Row 13: K1, p2, k11, p2, k1.

Row 14: P1, k2, p11, k2, p1.

Row 15: K1, p2, k3, k5 into next st; k3, k5 into next st; k3, p2, k1.

Row 16: P1, t3f, p2, k5 tog tbl; p3, k5 tog tbl; p2, t3b, p1.

Row 17: K2, p2, k9, p2, k2.

Row 18: P2, t3f, p7, t3b, p2.

Row 19: K3, p2, k3, k5 into next st, k3, p2, k3.

Row 20: P3, t3f, p2, k5 tog tbl; p2, t3b, p3.

Row 21: K4, p2, k5, p2, k4.

Row 22: P4, t3f, p3, t3b, p4.

Row 23: K5, p2, k3, p2, k5.

Row 24: P5, t3f, p1, t3b, p5.

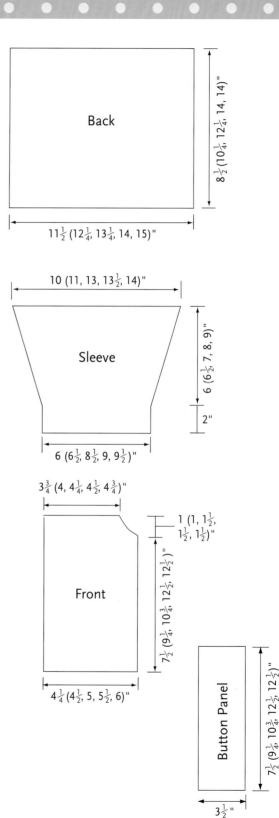

JACKET

Back

Using size 7 needles, CO 53 (55, 59, 63, 67) sts.
K 3 rows.

> **Next row (WS):** K1 (2, 3, 4, 5), *work first row of cable panel, k0 (0, 1, 2, 3)*; rep from * to * once, work first row of cable panel, end k1 (2, 3, 4, 5).

> **Next row (RS):** P1 (2, 3, 4, 5), *work second row of cable panel, p0 (0, 1, 2, 3)*; rep from * to * once, end p1 (2, 3, 4, 5).
> Cont as set, working the 3 cable panels with 1 (2, 3, 4, 5) st each end and 0 (0, 1, 2, 3) sts bet each panel worked in RSS as set. Work to the 3rd (14th, 2nd, 12th, 12th) row of the 3rd (3rd, 4th, 4th, 4th) vertical rep of cable panels [approx 8½ (10¼, 12¼, 14, 14) in. from bottom]. Put 1st 17 (18, 19, 20, 22) sts onto holder for 1 shoulder, then 19 (19, 21, 23, 23) sts onto 2nd holder for back neck, then rem 17 (18, 19, 20, 22) sts onto 3rd holder for the other shoulder. Set aside for later.

Left front

With size 7 needles, CO 19 (21, 23, 25, 27) sts.
K 3 rows.

> **Next row (WS):** K1 (2, 3, 4, 5), work first row of cable panel, k1 (2, 3, 4, 5).

> **Next row (RS):** P1 (2, 3, 4, 5), work second row cable panel, p1 (2, 3, 4, 5).
> Cont as set, working cable panel centered with 1 (2, 3, 4, 5) st on each end worked in RSS, until piece measures 7½ (9¼, 10¾, 12½, 12½) in. from beg, ending with a RS row.

> **Neck shaping:** BO 1 (2, 2, 3, 3) st beg of row (neck edge), and work in patt to end.
> Work one row even in patt.
> Cont to BO 1 st beg every WS row 1 (1, 2, 2, 2) time. Cont on rem 17 (18, 19, 20, 22) sts until the 3rd (14th, 2nd, 12th, 12th) row of the 3rd (3rd, 4th, 4th, 4th) vertical rep of cable panel [approx 8½ (10¼, 12¼, 14, 14) in. from bottom—same as back]. Put sts onto holder for later.

Right front

Work as for left front, reversing neck shaping.

Sleeves

With size 6 needles, CO 24 (26, 34, 36, 38) sts. Work in double rib as follows.

> **Row 1:** K2, p2 across, end k0 (2, 2, 0, 2).

> **Row 2:** P0 (2, 2, 0, 2), k2, p2 to end.
> Rep these 2 rows to 2 in., ending with a WS row. Change to size 7 needles and beg working in RSS, increasing 1 st each end on 1st row, then 1 st each end every 4th row 7 (8, 7, 5, 3) times, then 1 st each end every 6th row 0 (0, 1, 3, 5) times to 40 (44, 52, 54, 56) sts. Work without further shaping until sleeve measures 8 (8½, 9, 10, 11) in. from beg; BO.

Double-rib front panels

Button panel

With size 6 needles, CO 14 sts for all sizes. Work in double rib as for cuffs until piece measures 7½ (9¼, 10¾, 12½, 12½) in. BO in patt.

Buttonhole panel

Work as for first panel to 1¾ (2, 2, 3¼, 3¼) in., ending with a WS row.

> **Work buttonhole (RS):** K2, yo, p2tog, k2, p2, k2, yo, p2tog, k2. Cont in double rib as for first panel, working 2 more buttonhole rows as set at 4¼ (5¼, 6, 7½, 7½) in. and 6¾ (8½, 10, 11¾, 11¾) in. from bottom edge. Cont in double rib until piece measures same as first panel; BO.

Collar

Before working the collar, the shoulders need to be joined and the button panels sewn onto the fronts. Use the BO seam technique for shoulders as follows: With RSs facing each other, place the sts from the left front and left back each onto a size 7 dpn, and hold the needles parallel. Insert a third dpn into the first st on the first needle as if to k, then into the first st on the second needle as if to k, and k the 2 sts as 1. Rep this a second time—there should now be 2 sts on the right needle. *Pass the first st on the right needle over the second, and BO*. K the next 2 sts on the parallel dpn tog, and rep from * to *. Cont in this way, knitting the corresponding sts of each shoulder tog and binding off as you go, until 1 st rem. Break yarn, pull through last st to secure. Rep this process for right shoulder.

Sew the button panels onto the left and right fronts. If the sweater is for a girl, sew the buttonhole panel to the right front and for a boy, to the left front. Working from the WS, and starting at center top of left front button panel, use size 6 needle to pick up and k 15 (17, 18, 19, 21) sts up left front neck to shoulder seam. K across 19 (19, 21, 23, 23) sts on holder for back neck, increasing 1 st at center of back neck at the same time; then pick up and k 15 (17, 18, 19, 21) sts down right front neck, ending at center top of right front button panel—50 (54, 58, 62, 66) sts. Work in double rib as for cuffs and button panels for 3 1/4 in. BO in patt.

Finishing

Weave in loose ends. Center tops of the sleeves on shoulder seams with RSs facing each other, and backstitch in place. Sew side and sleeve seams, reversing seam at last 1 in. of cuff if you will be turning it up. Sew the six buttons opposite buttonholes, using thread to match one of the colors of the hat.

HAT

Body

With size 6 needles and A, CO 85 (93, 102) sts. Work 12 rows st st, increasing 8 sts evenly across last row to 93 (101, 110) sts. Change to B, and work stripe patt: *4 rows B, 2 rows A*; rep from * to * 3 (4, 5)

times. Work another 4 (5, 4) rows B to 4 (5, 5 3/4) in. from beg of stripe patt; BO.

Square top

With size 6 needles and A, CO 23 (25, 28) sts. Work in st st to 4 1/4 (4 1/2, 5) in.; BO.

Finishing

Weave in loose ends. Lightly press both hat pieces flat (except for rolled brim). Sew back seam of hat body, taking care to line up stripes, and reverse seam for rolled brim. Pin square piece to top edge of hat, matching back seam to center of one side of square. Using leftover chenille and a tapestry needle, stitch the square top to the hat body.

Tassels (make four)

Cut a piece of cardboard 2 1/4 in. Cut a 60-in. length of chenille, and wrap it around the cardboard form about 20 times. Cut end. With yarn still wrapped around cardboard, take another 10-in. length of chenille, and pull it through bottom edge bet cardboard and wrapped strands. Tie it tightly in a knot to secure bottom of tassel. Now insert a pair of scissors into the top edge bet cardboard and wrapped strands, and cut to free tassel from the cardboard. Cut another short length of chenille, and tie it around the strands about 1/2 in. above the tail. Pull ends of this piece into the strands of the tassel to hide it, and cut to match length of the tassel. Use tail to sew tassel to corner of the hat.

SHRINKING VIOLET

I came up with this set when I needed a dressy
cotton cardigan for one of my daughters to wear
to summer weddings. Of course at age 4, her favorite
colors were pink and purple, so purple it was.
Because it is worked in an easy eyelet flower pattern,
with very simple, minimal shaping, it's a good project
for an advanced beginner who's ready to try some slip-
stitch and yarn-over patterns. The picot-trimmed kerchief
is worked in stockinette stitch and can be finished
in about an hour. For more wardrobe versatility, try knitting
the entire outfit in white.

SHRINKING VIOLET

Eyelet Cardigan with Kerchief

∴ **MATERIALS**

Cardigan

3 (4, 5, 6, 8) 50g balls Dale of Norway Kolibri (100% Egyptian cotton, 114 yd./ball) in lavender #5135 (A) and 1 ball in ivory #0020 (B), or sport-weight yarn that will knit to the gauge given below
Size 5 (3.75mm) knitting needles, or size needed to match gauge given below
Size 3 (3.25mm) knitting needles
Set of size 5 dpns for knitting shoulder seams together
Stitch holders, row counter, tapestry needle
Size F (3.75mm) crochet hook
2 (2, 3, 3, 3) ¾-in. buttons
One snap

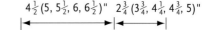

Kerchief

1 ball each A and B

Set

4 (5, 6, 7, 9) balls A, 1 ball B

∴ SIZES

0–3 months (6–9 months, 1–2 years, 3–4 years, 5–6 years)
Length: 9½ (11½, 13½, 14½, 15½) in.
Finished chest: 21 (25, 27, 31, 33) in.
Sleeve: 6 (7, 8½, 10½, 12½) in.
Kerchief: S (L)

∴ GAUGE

24 sts and 32 rows to 4 in./10cm over st st and eyelet patt on size 5 (3.75mm) needle
Don't waste precious time and precious yarn—make a gauge swatch before beginning!

∴ PATTERN STITCHES

Eyelet stitch pattern (multiple of 8 sts plus 5 sts)

Row 1 and all following WS rows: P.

Rows 2 and 6 (RS): K4, *ssk, yo, k1, yo, k2tog, k3*; rep from * to * across row, end k1.

Row 4: K5, *yo, sl2, k1, p2sso, yo, k5*; rep from * to * across.

Row 8: Ssk, yo, k1, yo, k2tog, *k3, ssk, yo, k1, yo, k2tog*; rep from * to * across row.

Row 10: K1, *yo, sl2, k1, p2sso, yo, k5*; rep from * to * across, end last rep with k1 instead of k5.

Row 12: Rep row 8.
Rep rows 1–12 for eyelet pattern.

Sl2, k1, p2sso: Sl next 2 sts tog (at same time) as if to k. K the next st. Pass the 2 sl sts tog (at the same time) over the k st and off the right needle.

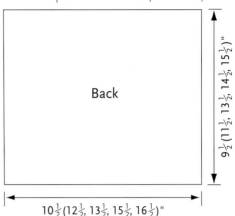

4½ (5, 5½, 6, 6½)"   2¾ (3¾, 4¼, 4¾, 5)"

Back

9½ (11½, 13½, 14½, 15½)"

10½ (12½, 13½, 15½, 16½)"

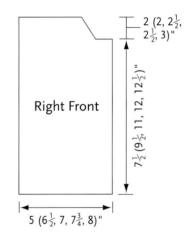

2 (2, 2½, 2½, 3)"

Right Front

7½ (9½, 11, 12, 12½)"

5 (6½, 7, 7¾, 8)"

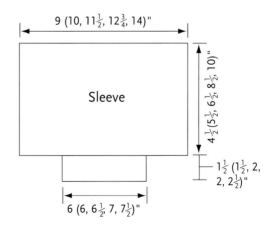

9 (10, 11½, 12¾, 14)"

Sleeve

4½ (5½, 6½, 8½, 10)"

1½ (1½, 2, 2, 2½)"

6 (6, 6½, 7, 7½)"

CARDIGAN

Back

With size 5 needles and A, sl on row counter, and CO 61 (77, 85, 93, 101) sts. Beg with row 1, work eyelet patt for approx 9½ (11½, 13½, 14½, 15½) in., ending with patt row 4, 6, 10, or 12 of rep (RS).

> **Next row (WS):** P across first 17 (23, 26, 29, 31) sts, and put on holder. BO center 27 (31, 33, 35, 39) sts purlwise for neck, p across rem 17 (23, 26, 29, 31) sts, and put on second holder for later. Make a note of row number you ended with.

Right front

With size 5 needle and A, CO 31 (39, 41, 47, 49) sts. Beg working eyelet patt with row 1, only beg patt rows 2 and 6 with k6 (6, 8, 6, 8) instead of k4; beg patt row 4 by k7 (7, 9, 7, 9) instead of k5; beg patt rows 8 and 12 by k2 (2, 4, 2, 4) before ssk; and beg patt row 10 by k3 (3, 5, 3, 5) instead of k1. Work with eyelet patt changes as established until right front measures approx 7½ (9½, 11, 12, 12½) in. from beg, or 16 (16, 20, 20, 24) rows fewer than the number of rows you ended the back with.

> **Shape neck (RS):** BO 10 sts knitwise beg this row; then dec 1 st beg every RS row, maintaining patt, 4 (6, 5, 8, 8) times to 17 (23, 26, 29, 31) sts. Cont without further shaping through same WS row as back, leaving sts on holder and leaving a 20-in. to 25-in. tail to k shoulder tog later.

Left front

With size 5 needle and A, CO 31 (39, 41, 47, 49) sts. Beg working eyelet patt with row 1, only end patt rows 2 and 6 by k3 (3, 5, 3, 5) instead of k1; end patt rows 4, 8, and 12 by k2 (2, 4, 2, 4); and end last rep of patt row 10 by k3 (3, 5, 3, 5). Work with eyelet patt changes as set until left front measures 7½ (9½, 11, 12, 12½) in. from beg, ending with a RS row.

> **Shape neck (WS):** BO 10 sts purlwise this row. Then dec 1 st by p2tog beg every WS row 4 (6, 5, 8, 8) times to 17 (23, 26, 29, 31) sts. Cont without further shaping, and finish as for right front, leaving a 20-in. to 25-in. tail.

Sleeves

With size 3 needles and A, CO 37 (37, 39, 43, 45) sts. Work in st st for 1½ (1½, 2, 2, 2½) in., ending with a WS row.

> **Next row (RS):** Change to size 5 needle, and inc 16 (24, 30, 34, 40) sts evenly across to 53 (61, 69, 77, 85) sts.

> **Next row (WS):** Beg working eyelet patt at row 1. Work in patt without further shaping until sleeve measures 6 (7, 8½, 10½, 12½) in. from beg, ending with row 4, 6, 10, or 12 of eyelet patt. BO all sts purlwise on WS, leaving a tail that is double the width of the top of the sleeve to be used to sew the sleeve to the body later.

Finishing

Ktog shoulder seams as follows: With RSs facing each other, place the sts from the left front and back shoulder each onto a size 5 dpn, and hold the two needles parallel to each other. Insert a third dpn into the first st on the first needle as if to k, then into the first st on the second needle as if to k, and k the 2 sts as one.

Rep this a second time—there should now be 2 sts on the right needle. *Pass the first st on the right needle over the second, and BO.* K the next set of sts on the parallel dpns together, and rep from * to *. Cont in this way, knitting the corresponding sts of each shoulder tog and binding off as you go, until 1 st remains on the right needle. Break yarn, and pull through last st to secure. Rep for right shoulder.

Weave in loose ends, except for those you will use to sew the seams. Steam all pieces, including shoulders seams. Center tops of sleeves on shoulder seams with RSs facing each other, and pin in place. Backstitch sleeves to body using the tails you left after binding off the sleeves. Sew inside sleeve seams and side seams. Lightly steam press over all.

Crocheted picot edgings: With crochet hook and B and starting on RS at lower right front side seam, work sc picot as follows: Work 1 sc, *chain four, insert the crochet hook back into same st, and pull up loop, yo, and pull yarn through both loops on hook (this reinserted chain is the picot); sc across next 3 sts*. Rep from * to * all the way across lower right front edge, up right front about 2½ (2½, 4–4½, 4–4½, 4–4½) in. before neck shaping begins, and you have just finished three single crochets, work 2 (2, 3, 3, 3) button loops as follows: **Chain six (button loop), reinsert hook back into same st, and pull up loop. Yo and pull yarn through both loops on hook, sc in next 3 sts, chain four (picot), reinsert hook back into same st, sc over next 3 sts**. Rep from ** to ** 0 (0, 1, 1, 1) more times, chain six (neck edge button loop), reinsert hook back into same st.
Cont working picot as established before button loops around neck and remainder of body back to where you began. Pull yarn through last st, and weave in end.
Work crocheted picot trim around cuffs of both sleeves, starting and ending at the seams.
Sew buttons on left front opposite the 2 (2, 3, 3, 3) button loops, about 1 in. or 2 in. in from edge (depending on size of child). Sew one side of snap to neck edge on left front RS, and then sew the other part of the snap on WS of right front so that

if you have a large overlap of right front over left front, the left front won't flap around underneath.

KERCHIEF

With size 5 needles and A, CO 77 (95) sts. P one row.

Next row (RS): Ssk, k across to last 2 sts, k2tog.

Next row (WS): P even.
Rep these last two rows, dec 1 st at each end as established every RS row until 3 sts remain, ending with a WS row.

Next row (RS): Ssk, k1.

Next row (WS): P2tog. Cut yarn, and pull through this last st. Weave in the loose ends, and steam the triangle.
Work crocheted picot edging in B around perimeter of kerchief, as you did for the cardigan.

Chin ties: With crochet hook and B, pull up a loop at the corner on the longest side, and work chain for 12 in. Pull through last st, and tighten. Use a tapestry needle to weave this end back in and out of chain to hide it. Rep for second tie at the other end of the longest side of the kerchief.

TWEEDY PIE

This was the first Monkeysuit I designed,
and it's still one of my favorites—and one of the most popular.
The red and green color combination is one I'm drawn
to over and over again. I actually have to stop myself
from making everything orange-red and lime green.
At first, I really wanted to make this coat for myself.
Realizing that I'd probably never see it finished, I decided
to knit it on a small scale for my daughter Isabel.
That's the beauty of knitting for babies and children:
The projects go so quickly, it's not unrealistic to expect
to finish them in a month or even less.

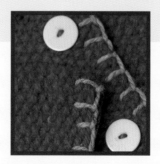

TWEEDY PIE

Seed Stitch Swing Coat with Matching Hat and Mittens

❖ MATERIALS

4 (5, 5, 6) 100g skeins Rowan Magpie Tweed (185 yd./170m per skein) in Sienna #766 (A) and 1 (1, 1, 1) skein in Pesto #768, or yarn that will knit to the gauge given below
Three 1-in. buttons and one ⅝-in. button
Pair of size 8 (5mm) knitting needles, or size needed to match coat gauge given below
Size 8 circ needle for picking up collar sts
Set of size 8 dpns for working shoulder seams
Set of size 5 (3.75mm) dpns, or size needed to match mitten gauge given below
Crochet hook for mitten chain, hat tie, and button loop at neck edge
Tapestry needle, stitch holders

❖ SIZES

1 (2, 3, 4) year
Length: 15 (16½, 18, 19½) in.
Chest: 23 (25, 27, 29) in.
Sleeve: 9½ (10, 10½, 11) in. (cuff will be turned up 1½ in.)
Hat circumference: 17 (17½, 18, 19½) in.

❖ GAUGE

16 sts and 27 rows to 4 in. or 10cm in seed st on size 8 needles
Don't waste precious time and precious yarn—make a gauge swatch before beginning!

❖ PATTERN STITCHES

Seed stitch

> **Row 1:** *K1, p1; rep from * to end of row.

> **Row 2:** *P1, k1; rep from * to end of row.
> Note: All pieces are worked entirely in seed st.

SWING COAT

Back

Using size 8 needles and A, CO 72 (80, 84, 92) sts. Beg seed st, and work 5 rows.

> **Next row (RS):** K2tog, work to last 2 sts, k2tog. Dec 1 st each end every sixth row 4 (8, 6, 10) times and then every eighth row 3 (1, 3, 1) times

to 56 (60, 64, 68) sts. Work until piece measures 9 (10, 11, 12) in. from beg.

BO 4 sts beg next 2 rows for armholes—48 (52, 56, 60) sts. Work even until armhole measures 6 (6½, 7, 7½) in.

Work 15 (16, 17, 18) sts for shoulder, and place on holder. Work next 18 (20, 22, 24) sts, and place on second holder for neck. Work remaining 15 (16, 17, 18) sts, and place on third holder for second shoulder.

Right front

With size 8 needles and A, CO 36 (40, 42, 46) sts. Work as for back, only shape side ending RS rows, and shape armhole beg WS row. At the same time, work buttonholes on RS rows—first buttonhole 6½ (7½, 8½, 9½) in. from bottom, second buttonhole 9½ (10¾, 12, 13¼) in. from bottom, and third 12½ (14, 15½, 17) in. from bottom—as follows: Patt 3 sts, p2tog, yo, patt to end. Work until front measures 13½ (15, 16½, 18) in., and you have 24 (26, 28, 30) sts, ending with a WS row.

Neck shaping: BO 6 (7, 8, 9) sts beg this RS row (neck edge), and work to end. Work 1 row even. BO 2 sts at neck edge, and work to end. Work 1 row even. BO 1 st at neck edge—15 (16, 17, 18) sts. Work until front measures 15 (16½, 18, 19½) in. as back. Place these shoulder sts on holder to be finished later.

Left front

Work as for right front, reversing side and neck shaping, and eliminating buttonholes.

Sleeves

With size 8 needles and A, CO 32 (34, 36, 40) sts. Work in seed st for 3 in., ending with a WS row. Inc 1 st each end next row. Then inc 1 st each end every fourth row 4 (5, 6, 5) times and then every sixth row 3 (3, 3, 4) times to 48 (52, 56, 60) sts. Work until sleeve measures 9½ (10, 10½, 11) in.; BO.

Collar

Before working the collar, the shoulders need to be joined. Use the BO seam technique for shoulder seams as follows: With RSs facing each other, place

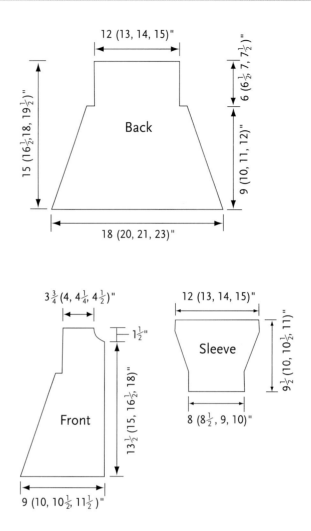

the sts from the left front and back shoulder each onto a size 8 dpn, and hold the needles parallel. Insert a third dpn into the first st on the first needle as if to k, then into the first st on the second needle as if to k, and k the 2 sts as one. Rep this a second time—there should now be 2 sts on the right needle. *Pass the first st on the right needle over the second, and BO*. K the next 2 sts on the parallel dpn tog, and rep from * to *. Cont in this way, knitting the corresponding sts of each shoulder tog and binding off as you go, until 1 st remains on the right needle. Break yarn, and pull through last st to secure. Rep this process for right shoulder. Lightly steam press seams.

Now you are ready to work the collar. With WS facing and B, and starting 1 in. in from neck shaping, pick up and k 10 (11, 12, 13) sts up left front neck to shoulder seam; work across the 18 (20, 22, 24) sts from holder for back neck, and then pick up and k 10 (11, 12, 13) sts down right front neck, leaving 1 in. at neck edge—38 (42, 46, 50) sts. Beg seed st, and work 4 rows.

Next row, inc 1 st each end. Then inc 1 st each end every third row 3 (4, 4, 5) times—46 (52, 56, 62) sts. Work even until collar measures 3 (3½, 4, 4) in. BO in patt. Lightly steam collar seam.

Pockets (make two)

CO 16 (18, 20, 20) sts in A. Work in seed st until pocket measures 4 (4½, 4¾, 5) in. BO in patt. Blanket st the top edge of the pockets in B.

Finishing

Weave in loose ends. Gently press and steam pieces.

Attach sleeves: Center sleeve on armhole, and backstitch sleeve top to armhole edge with RSs facing each other, sewing the bound-off stitches at armhole edges to the straight side edge at the top of the sleeve. Sew the sleeve and side seams. Lightly steam seams.

Make button loop at right neck edge as follows:
With the crochet hook and A, and starting a few sts down from the top neck edge, sc 2, up to corner of neck edge. Now chain 6 sts to form loop, reattach where you left off, and work 2 more sc toward collar. Pull yarn through, and secure. Sew the three large buttons opposite buttonholes. Sew the small button underneath collar opposite the button loop. With B, work blanket st along front openings, hem, and cuffs. Button up the coat, and lay it out flat to pin pockets 3 (3¼, 3½, 4) in. up from bottom, centered on left and right fronts. Sew pockets in place.

HAT

This hat is a piece of cake—just a big rectangle with the top corners tied together.

With size 8 needles and A, CO 68 (70, 72, 78) sts. Work in seed st until piece measures 8 (8½, 9, 9½) in.; BO. Fold piece in half width-wise, and sew top and side seams, reversing seam on lower 1½ in. for turned-up edge. Using crochet hook and B, draw up a loop through hat top corner, and work chain st for 7 in. Cut yarn, and pull end through last loop. Rep for other corner. Tie cords in a bow, bringing the hat corners together. Blanket st bottom ws edge of hat in B, and turn up.

MITTENS
[Two Sizes–1(2-3) year]

Right mitten

With size 5 dpn and B, CO 25 (27) sts. Divide sts evenly onto 3 dpn with 8 (9) sts each on first and second needles and 9 (9) sts on third. Join rnd without twisting, and work in seed st for 1¾ (2) in. Sl first 5 (6) sts from first needle onto holder for thumb.

Next rnd: CO 5 (6) sts. Patt to end of rnd.
Cont mitten body in seed st until mitten measures 3¼ (3½) in., and next rnd will beg with a k st.

Shape top: (First size only—second size follows.)

Next rnd: *K1, p3tog, k1, p1, k1, p1*. Rep from * to * twice, k1—19 sts.
Work three rnds even.

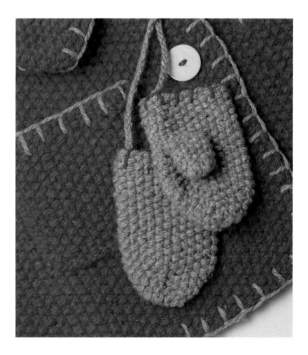

Next rnd: *K1, p3tog, k1, p1*. Rep from * to * twice, k1—13 sts.
Work one rnd even.

Next rnd: *K1, p3tog*. Rep from * to * twice, k1—7 sts. Break yarn, leaving a long enough tail to work last row, pull yarn through sts as they are worked. Pull up and secure.

Shape top: (Second size.)

Next rnd: First needle—k1, p3tog, k1, p1, k1, p1, k1. Second needle—p1, k3tog, p1, k1, p1, k1, p1. Third needle—as first needle—21 sts.
Work three rnds even.

Next rnd: First needle—k1, p3tog, k1, p1, k1. Second needle—p1, k3tog, p1, k1, p1. Third needle—as first needle—15 sts.
Work one rnd even.

Next rnd: First needle—k1, p3tog, k1. Second needle—p1, k3tog, p1. Third needle—as first needle—9 sts. Break yarn, leaving a long enough tail to work last row, pull yarn through sts as they are worked. Pull up and secure.

Thumb (both sizes): Put 5 (6) sts from holder onto 2 dpns, and pick up and k 6 (7) sts from bound off edge in palm. Divide sts evenly onto the 3 dpns, and work in seed st to 1¼ (1¾) in. Break off yarn, leaving a long enough tail to pull through sts as last rnd is worked. Pull up and secure.

Left mitten

Work body as for right mitten to 3¼ (3½) in. and to a rnd that will beg with a k st.

Shape top: (First size only.)

Next rnd: *K1, p1, k1, p1, k3tog, p1*. Rep from * to * twice, k1—19 sts.
Work three rnds even.

Next rnd: *K1, p1, k3tog, p1*. Rep from * to * twice, k1—13 sts.
Work one rnd.

Next rnd: *K3tog, p1*. Rep from * to * twice, k1—7 sts. Break yarn, and pull it through st by st. Pull up and secure.

Shape top: (Second size.)

Next rnd: First needle—k1, p1, k1, p1, k1, p3tog, k1. Second needle—p1, k1, p1, k1, p1, k3tog, p1. Third needle—as first needle—21 sts.
Work three rnds even.

Next rnd: First needle—k1, p1, k1, p3tog, k1. Second needle—p1, k1, p1, k3tog, p1. Third needle—as first needle—15 sts.
Work one rnd even.

Next rnd: First needle—k1, p1, k3tog. Second needle—p1, k1, p3tog. Third needle—as first needle—9 sts. Break yarn, and pull through and secure as you did with the other mitten.

Thumb (both sizes): Work thumb as you did for right mitten.

Finishing: Weave in ends, and work blanket st in A along cuff edge. With crochet needle and B, make a mitten chain using a single chain st to desired length (approx 20 in. to 30 in.). Sew chain ends to inside edges of mittens.

RED, SET, GO

I made this set in the newborn size for
my daughter Matilda to wear home from the hospital.
Granted, something knit in a newborn size will not fit
for very long, but this set is so easy to make—it can be made
in a weekend—it's worth it. Matilda was on the small side,
and born in March, so she was able to wear hers
until summer. I did try to put it on her when she was
about 7 months old, hoping that it might have
grown with her, and it looked like a very fashionable
shrug. My sister made this set in an ivory color,
which also looks lovely.

RED, SET, GO

Seed Stitch Crossover Cardigan with Hat and Booties

Cardigan

3 (4, 5, 6, 6, 7, 8) 50g balls Muench Yarns/GGH GOA (50% cotton, 50% acrylic, 66 yd. per ball) in red #7, or other chunky yarn that will knit to the gauge given below

Size 8 (5mm) knitting needles, or size needed to match gauge given below

Three size 8 dpns

Four stitch holders, row counter, tapestry needle, and markers

Two ⅞-in. buttons

Hat

2 balls GOA

One ⅝-in. button

Booties

1 ball GOA

Size 7 (4.5mm) and size 8 (5mm) needles

Set

6 (6, 7, 8, 9, 10, 11) balls GOA

∴ SIZES

Sweater: Newborn (3, 6, 9–12, 18, 24, 36 months)

Length: 8 (9, 10, 11, 12, 12½, 13½) in.

Chest: 19 (20½, 22, 24½, 26½, 28, 30) in.

Sleeve: 5 (6, 6¾, 7½, 8½, 9½, 10½) in.

Hat sizes: Newborn (3, 6, 12, 24–36 months)

Bootie sizes: Newborn (3, 6 months)

∴ GAUGE

Generic yarn gauge: 14 sts and 20 rows to 4 in. (10cm) over st st on size 8 needles

Seed st gauge: 14 sts and 24 rows to 4 in. on size 8 needles

Don't waste precious time and precious yarn—make a gauge swatch before beginning!

∴ PATTERN STITCHES

Seed st over an odd number of sts.

All rows: K1, *p1, k1; rep from * to end.

Seed st over an even number of sts.

Row 1 (RS): *K1, p1; rep from * to end.

Row 2: *P1, k1; rep from * to end.

CARDIGAN

Back

With size 8 needles, CO 33 (36, 39, 43, 47, 49, 53) sts. Work in seed st for 8 (9, 10, 11, 12, 12½, 13½) in., ending with a WS row.

Next row: Patt across first 9 (10, 12, 13, 15, 15, 16) sts, and put on holder. BO center 15 (16, 15, 17, 17, 19, 21) sts in patt for neck, patt across rem 9 (10, 12, 13, 15, 15, 16) sts; put on second holder.

Left front

With size 8 needles, CO 11 (12, 13, 15, 17, 17, 19) sts.

Shape opening: Inc 1 st at end of first (RS) row and then 1 st ending every RS row 8 (8, 10, 10, 9, 11, 10) more times, working new sts into patt, to 20 (21, 24, 26, 27, 29, 30) sts. From here, shape as follows: Inc 1 st at end of every fourth row 4 (5, 0, 0, 0, 0, 0) times and then every sixth row 0 (0, 4, 4, 5, 5, 6) times to 24 (26, 28, 30, 32, 34, 36) sts. If the sweater is for a girl, work without further shaping until left front measures 6½ (7, 8, 9, 9½, 10, 11) in. from beg, ending with a WS row. Skip ahead to neck shaping.
If the sweater is for a boy, work without further shaping until left front measures 5¾ (6¼, 7¼, 8¼, 8¾, 9¼, 10¼) in. from beg, ending with a WS row.

Next row (RS)—work buttonholes: Patt 12 (13, 15, 17, 18, 20, 21) sts, k2tog, yo, patt 5 (6, 6, 6, 7, 7, 8) sts, k2tog, yo, patt 3.

Next row (WS): Patt across as usual.
Cont in patt until piece measures 6½ (7, 8, 9, 9½, 10, 11) in. from beg, ending with a WS row.

Shape neck (RS): Patt across to last 2 sts, work 2 sts tog in patt.

Row 2: Work 2tog in patt, patt to end.

Row 3: Rep first neck shaping row—21 (23, 25, 27, 29, 31, 33) sts.

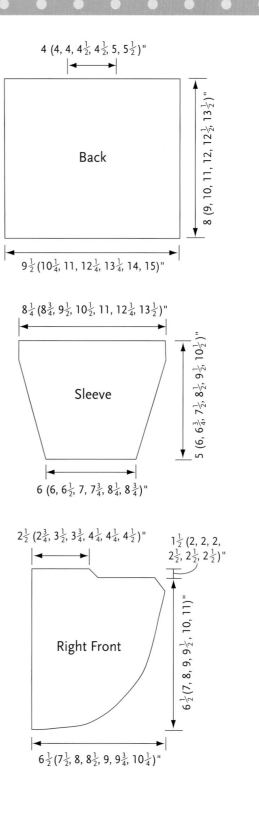

4 (4, 4, 4½, 4½, 5, 5½)"

Back

8 (9, 10, 11, 12, 12½, 13½)"

9½ (10¼, 11, 12¼, 13¼, 14, 15)"

8¼ (8¾, 9½, 10½, 11, 12¼, 13½)"

Sleeve

5 (6, 6¾, 7½, 8½, 9½, 10½)"

6 (6, 6½, 7, 7¾, 8¼, 8¾)"

2½ (2¾, 3½, 3¾, 4¼, 4¼, 4½)"

1½ (2, 2, 2, 2½, 2½, 2½)"

Right Front

6½ (7, 8, 9, 9½, 10, 11)"

6½ (7½, 8, 8½, 9, 9¾, 10¼)"

Sleeves

With size 8 needle, CO 21 (21, 23, 25, 27, 29, 31) sts. Beg with a RS row, work in seed st for 2 rows.

Next row (RS)—beg shaping: Inc 1 st at each end of this row, then every sixth row 1 (2, 0, 1, 0, 0, 1) time, then every eighth row 2 (2, 4, 4, 5, 6, 6) times to 29 (31, 33, 37, 39, 43, 47) sts. Cont without further shaping until sleeve measures 5 (6, 6¾, 7½, 8½, 9½, 10½) in. BO in patt, leaving a tail twice the length of the width of the sleeve top to sew sleeve to sweater later.

Finishing

Use the BO seam technique for shoulder seams as follows: With RSs facing each other, place the sts from the left front and back shoulder each onto a size 8 dpn, and hold the needles parallel. Insert a third dpn into the first st on the first needle as if to k, then into the first st on the second needle as if to k, and k the 2 sts as one. Rep this a second time— there should now be 2 sts on the right needle. *Pass the first st on the right needle over the second, and BO*. K the next 2 sts on the parallel dpns tog, and rep from * to *. Cont in this way, knitting the corresponding sts of each shoulder tog and binding off as you go, until 1 st remains on the right needle. Break yarn, pull through last st to secure. Rep this process for right shoulder.

Weave in loose ends, except for those that will be used to sew seams. Lightly steam pieces to block, including shoulder seams.

Attach sleeves: Center sleeve on armhole, and backstitch sleeve top to armhole edge with RSs facing each other. Sew sleeve and side seams, and lightly steam. Sew buttons opposite buttonholes.

HAT

With size 8 needles, CO 19 (21, 23, 25, 27) sts. Work 4 rows seed st.

Next row (RS)—beg shaping: Inc 1 st at the end of this row, then 1 st at the end of every fourth row 7 (6, 4, 5, 4) times, then every sixth row 0 (0, 3, 0, 0) times, and then every eighth row 0 (1, 0, 2, 3) times, working new sts into patt, to 27 (29, 31, 33, 35) sts.

Row 4 (WS): BO first 9 (10, 10, 11, 11, 13, 14) sts in patt, and patt to end—12 (13, 15, 16, 18, 18, 19) sts.

Next row: Work 2tog in patt at neck edge every row 3 more times to 9 (10, 12, 13, 15, 15, 16) sts. Work without further shaping until left front measures same as back. Leave sts on holder, leaving a 15-in. to 25-in. tail to k shoulder seam tog later.

Right front

Work as for left front, reversing shaping, and eliminating buttonholes if the sweater is for a boy.

For a girl, work buttonholes as follows: Work until piece measures 5¾ (6¼, 7¼, 8¼, 8¾, 9¼, 10¼) in. from beg, ending with a WS row.

Next (buttonhole row): Patt 3, yo, k2tog, patt 5 (6, 6, 6, 7, 7, 8), k2tog, yo, patt to end.

Next row (WS): Patt across as usual.
Cont in patt until piece measures 6½ (7, 8, 9, 9½, 10, 11) in. from beg, ending with a RS row. Shape neck, and finish as for left front, only beg shaping on WS.

Work next row (WS) even.

Next row—shape left back: Dec 1 st at the end of this row, then 1 st at the end of every eighth row 0 (1, 0, 2, 3) times, then every sixth row 0 (0, 3, 0, 0) times, and then every fourth row 7 (6, 4, 5, 4) times to 19 (21, 23, 25, 27) sts. Work four more rows seed st. BO sts in patt.

Finishing: Fold hat in half lengthwise with RSs facing each other so that the shaped sides are lined up to make a point. Backstitch seam along shaped edge. Weave in loose ends.

Neckband/chin strap: With size 7 needle and RS facing, pick up and k 37 (39, 42, 46, 50) sts along bottom edge (cast-on and bound-off edges), and then CO an additional 12 (13, 13, 14, 14) sts for chin strap—49 (52, 55, 60, 64) sts. Work 4 rows seed st.

Next row (WS)—work buttonhole: Patt 3, yo, k2tog, patt to end.
Work four more rows seed st, binding off loosely in patt on last row. Weave in loose ends. Sew button on neckband opposite buttonhole.

Booties

With size 7 needle, CO 18 (22, 26) sts. Work 8 rows seed st, beg with a RS row. Change to size 8 needles, and cont in seed st as established for 3 more rows.

Next row (WS): P.

Next row (RS)—work eyelet row for tie: K2 *k2tog, yo, k2*; rep from * to * across to last 4 sts, end k2tog, yo, k2.

Next row (WS): P.

Next row: K 6 (8, 10), work seed st over next 6 sts, and k 6 (8, 10).

Next row (WS): P 6 (8, 10), work seed st over next 6 sts, and p 6 (8, 10). Rep the last 2 rows 1 (2, 3) more time. Cut yarn.

Next row (RS): Sl first 6 (8, 10) sts onto holder, rejoin yarn, work in established seed st across next 6 instep sts, and then place rem 6 (8, 10) sts on second holder.

Work instep: Turn and cont in seed st on the 6 instep sts for 9 (11, 13) more rows, ending with a WS row. Cut yarn, and leave instep sts on needle. Sl 6 (8, 10) sts from first holder back to needle, ready to beg RS. K across these sts, and then pick up and k 7 (8, 9) sts along length of instep. K across the 6 instep sts, then pick up and k 7 (8, 9) sts along the length of the other side of the instep, and then k across rem 6 (8, 10) sts from second holder—32 (38, 44) sts. Beg with a p row, work 3 rows st st.

Next (RS)—shape sole: K1, k2tog, k 10 (13, 16), k2tog, k2, k2tog, k10 (13, 16), k2tog, k1.

Next (WS): P1, p2tog, p 8 (11, 14), p2tog, p2, p2tog, p 8 (11, 14), p2tog, p1—24 (30, 36) sts. BO sts. Weave in ends. Sew back and sole seam, reversing for folded-over edge at ankle.

Make tie: Chain st for 16 (18, 20) in. Weave ends of chain back into chain to conceal, or fray ends to form a mini-tassel. Weave tie in and out of eyelets, and tie in a bow.

GREEN SLEEVES

The sweater in this set was inspired by
those painting smocks we used to wear in kindergarten.
The pocket and collar are knit separately and sewn
on, making this an easy sweater for a beginner. The pants
are also easy—made up of two identical halves that are
then sewn together with an elastic inserted into the waistband.
At 4 stitches to the inch, both the sweater and pants work
up very quickly. My version is done in cotton, but if you're
knitting just the sweater, a chunky wool would work very
nicely for a warm fall or winter sweater, with plenty
of pocket room for your little one to store "treasures."

GREEN SLEEVES

Unisex Pullover with Striped Collar and Pocket and Matching Pants

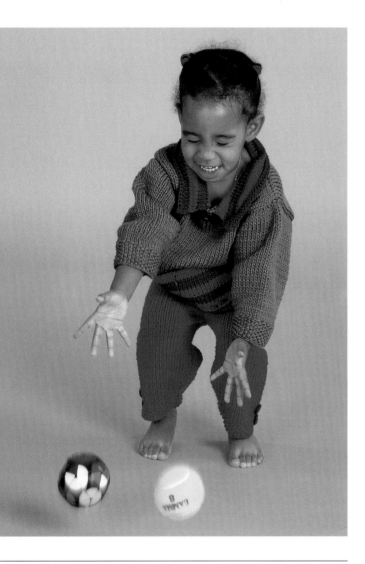

∴ MATERIALS

Pullover

6 (7, 7, 8, 10) 50g balls Crystal Palace Monterey Cotton (70 yd./skein) in green #033 (A), 1 ball each in red #76 (B) and blue #06 (C), or yarn that will knit to the gauge given below
One 1-in. button for neck
Size 7 (4.5mm) needles
Size 9 (5.5mm) knitting needles, or size needed to match gauge given below
Set of size 9 dpns for shoulder seams
Tapestry needle and stitch holders

Pants

5 (6, 8) balls B
Size 7 and 9 needles
1 yd. elastic for waistband
Four ¾-in. buttons for cuffs

∴ SIZES

Pullover: 1 (2, 3, 4, 5) year
Pants: 12–18 months (2–3, 4–5 years)
Pullover length: 14 (15, 16, 17, 18) in.
Chest: 22 (24, 28, 30) in.
Sleeve: 8 (9, 10, 11, 12) in.
Pants (waist to cuff length): 16 (19, 22) in.

∴ GAUGE

16 sts and 22 rows to 4 in./10cm over st st on size 9 needles
Don't waste precious time and precious yarn—make a gauge swatch before beginning!

∴ PATTERN STITCHES

Seed st over an odd number of sts.

All rows: K1, *p1, k1; rep from * to end.

Seed st over an even number of sts.

Row 1 (RS): *K1, p1; rep from * to end.

Row 2: *P1, k1; rep from * to end.

PULLOVER

Back

Using size 7 needles and A, CO 52 (56, 60, 64, 68) sts. Work in seed st for ¾ in., ending with a RS row. Change to size 9 needles.

Next row: Seed st 4, p across row to last 4 sts, seed st 4.

Next row: Seed st 4, k across row to last 4 sts, seed st 4.
Rep these last two rows once more.

Next row (WS): Beg with a k row, and work all sts in st st until back measures 7½ (8, 8½, 9, 9½) in. from beg.

Shape armhole: BO 4 sts beg next 2 rows to 44 (48, 52, 56, 60) sts. Work until armhole measures 6½ (7, 7½, 8, 8½) in. Work first 11 (12, 14, 15, 16) sts, and put on holder for later. BO center 22 (24, 24, 26, 28) sts for neck, work rem 11 (12, 14, 15, 16) sts, and put on holder, leaving a 20-in. tail to knit shoulder seams tog later.

Front

Work as for back until front measures 12½ (13½, 14½, 15½, 16½) in. from beg.

Shape neck: Work first 14 (15, 17, 18, 19) sts, join second ball of yarn, BO center 16 (18, 18, 20, 22) sts for neck, and work rem 14 (15, 17, 18, 19) sts. Working both sides at the same time, BO 1 st at each neck edge 3 times (over 6 rows) until 11 (12, 14, 15, 16) sts rem on each shoulder. Work until front measures same as back, and put each set of shoulder sts onto holders for finishing later.

Sleeves

With size 7 needles and A, CO 32 (34, 36, 38, 40) sts. Work in seed st for 14 rows (2 in.). Change to size 9 needles.

Next row (RS): Beg st st, and inc 1 st each end this row, then every other row 5 (5, 5, 4, 4) times, and then every fourth row 4 (5, 6, 8, 9) times to 52 (56, 60, 64, 68) sts. Cont without further shaping until sleeve measures 8 (9, 10, 11, 12) in. from beg; BO sts.

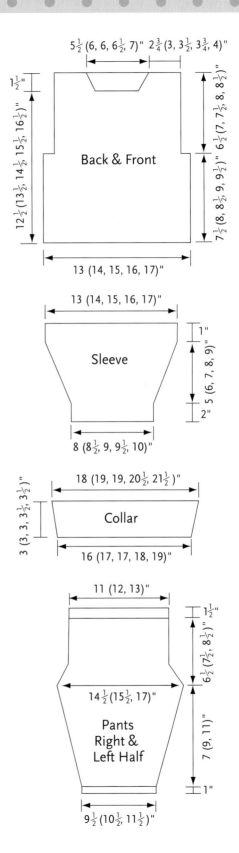

84) sts. Work 0 (0, 0, 1, 1) more stripes in B, increasing in third row of stripe as before—72 (76, 76, 82, 86) sts. BO loosely.

Pocket

Pocket is also worked entirely in st st. With size 9 needles and B, CO 32 (36, 40, 44, 48) sts. *Work 4 rows. Change to C, and work 4 rows*. Rep from * to * 1 (1, 1, 2, 2) time. Work 4 more rows B. BO loosely.

Finishing

Join shoulders: Use the BO seam technique for shoulder seams as follows: With RSs facing each other, place the sts from the left front and back shoulder each onto a size 9 dpn, and hold the two needles parallel to each other. Insert a third dpn into the first st on the first needle as if to k, then into the first st on the second needle as if to k, and k the 2 sts as 1. Rep this a second time—there should now be 2 sts on the right needle. *Pass the first st on the right needle over the second, and BO.* K the next set of sts on the parallel dpns together, and rep from * to *. Cont in this way, knitting the corresponding sts of each shoulder together and binding off as you go, until 1 st rem on the right needle. Break yarn, pull through last st to secure. Rep this process for right shoulder. Weave in all loose ends. Lightly steam press shoulder seams and all other pieces.

Attach sleeves: Center sleeve on armhole with RSs facing each other, and pin in place. Backstitch sleeve top to armhole edge, sewing the bound-off sts at armhole edges to the straight side edge at the top of the sleeve. Sew inside sleeve seams. Sew side seams, leaving 1½ in. at hem open for side slits.

Attach collar and pocket: Pin collar to neck opening with RS of collar facing WS of sweater, centering collar ends at center front neck. Backstitch in place, and turn out to right side. Center pocket on front bet side seams 1½ (1¾, 2, 2, 2) in. up from bottom, and pin in place. Using a double strand of A, topstitch pocket to front down one side,

Collar

Collar is worked entirely in st st. With size 9 needles and B, CO 64 (68, 68, 72, 76) sts. *Work 2 rows.

Row 3 B (inc): K1, m1, k across row until 1 st rem, m1, k1.

Row 4 B: P even to complete stripe in B. Change to C, and work two rows.

Row 3 C: Inc as you did for third row B.

Row 4 C: P even to complete stripe in C*. Change back to B. Rep from * to * 1 time—72 (76, 76, 80,

across bottom, and up the other side. Then top-stitch a vertical line up the center of the pocket, thereby dividing the pocket into two compartments. Sew button at center front neck, using a single ply of color B. Lightly steam all seams.

PANTS

Right half

Cuff (in 2 parts): With size 7 needles and B, CO 19 (21, 23) sts. Work in seed st for 7 rows (1 in.). Put sts onto holder. Make another identical piece. Put sts from both cuff pieces onto size 9 needle, and beg on WS, p 1 row, joining the 2 cuff pieces at the center (this will form the side slit)—38 (42, 46) sts.
Beg with a k row, work from here in st st, and inc 1 st each end this row, then 1 st each end every other row 5 (2, 1) times, and then every sixth row 4 (7, 9) times to 58 (62, 68) sts. Work until leg measures 7 (9, 11) in. from beg st st, ending with a WS row.

Shape crotch: BO 3 sts beg next 2 rows, then BO 1 st beg next 8 (8, 10) rows to 44 (48, 52) sts. Cont without further shaping until piece measures 6½ (7½, 8½) in. above crotch—14½ (17½, 20½) in. total.

Waistband: Change to size 7 needles, and work seed st for 1½ in., ending with a WS row. P 1 RS row for turning waistband hem. P next WS row, and beg with a k row, cont in st st for 1½ in. BO all sts.

Left half
Make identical to right half.

Finishing
Weave in all loose ends. Lightly steam press both pieces. Sew front and back crotch-to-waist seams, including turned waistband hem. Sew inside leg seams. Fold over waistband hem to inside, and lightly steam press in place. Lightly steam press crotch to waist and inside leg seams while you're at it. Pin turned waistband in place, and whipstitch around,

leaving a few inches open to insert elastic. Attach a safety pin to one end of elastic, and thread elastic through waistband. Cut to desired length (an inch or two shorter than the child's waist should do), and sew ends together. Whipstitch hem opening closed. Separate a strand of B into a few ply, and use a single ply to sew two buttons centered one on top of the other on the side of each leg just above the side slit opening. You may want to reinforce the side slits where they split off, because they will want to pull apart over time.

YELLOW JACKET

People love to dress babies as animals, fruit,
and even insects. This yellow and black striped cardigan
and bumble bee hat, all with picot edging, can double
as a Halloween costume. My daughter Matilda wore it
for her first Halloween outing when she was about
7 months old. This set is knit in baby yarn, but it's a
double strand, so you can finish it before the baby gets old
enough not to want to be seen in such a costume.
Change the color combination, and it's no longer a bee.
I recently received a picture from a knitter who made it up
in blue and white, and the effect was dramatically different.

YELLOW JACKET

Striped, Picot-Edged Cardigan with Bumblebee Hat

∴ **MATERIALS**

Cardigan

3 (3, 3, 4, 5) 50g balls Dale of Norway Baby Ull (Superwash Wool, 175m per ball) in black #0090 (A) and 2 (2, 2, 2, 3) balls in yellow #2015 (B), or yarn that will knit to the gauge given below
5 (7, 7, 7, 7) ⅝-in. buttons to match A
Size 5 (3.75mm) knitting needles for button bands
Size 7 (4.5mm) knitting needles, or size needed to match gauge given below
One set size 7 dpns for shoulder seams
Size 5 circ needle for picking up collar stitches
Row counter, tapestry needle, and stitch holders
Note: Yarn is used double throughout.

Hat

1 ball each A and B
Size 5 knitting needles
Size 7 knitting needles
One set size 5 dpns for I-cord
1-in. to 1¼-in. commercial pom-pom maker

Set

3 (4, 4, 5, 6) balls A and 2 (2, 3, 3, 3) balls B—with a small hat for first two sizes, a medium hat for third size, and a large hat for last two sizes

∴ **SIZES**

0–3 (3–6, 9–12, 12–24, 24–36) months
Length: 9½ (10¼, 11, 12, 13) in.
Chest: 20 (22, 24, 27, 29) in.
Sleeve: 6½ (7¼, 8, 9, 10) in.
Hat circumference: S-15 (M-17½, L-19¼) in.

∴ **GAUGE**

19 sts and 26 rows to 4 in./10cm over st st on size 7 needles with baby yarn used double
Don't waste precious time and precious yarn—make a gauge swatch before beginning!

∴ **PATTERN STITCHES**

Stripe pattern
4 rows A, 4 rows B in st st

CARDIGAN

Back

Using size 5 needles and 2 strands A, CO 48 (52, 58, 64, 68) sts.

Work picot hem: Work six rows st st.

Next row (eyelet turning row—RS): K1 *k2tog, yo*; rep from * to * across, end k1.
P one row.
Still using A, beg stripe patt (four rows A, four rows B, in st st). Change to larger needles when you finish first black stripe. Cont with patt as set until back measures 4¾ (5¼, 5½, 6, 6¾) in. from eyelet row.

Shape armhole: BO 4 sts beg next 2 rows, and cont in stripe patt until back measures 9½ (10¼, 11, 12, 13) in. from eyelet row, ending with a half or full stripe. Put first 10 (12, 14, 17, 18) sts onto a holder, put center 20 (20, 22, 22, 24) sts onto a second holder for neck, and put rem 10 (12, 14, 17, 18) sts onto third holder for later.

Left front

With size 5 needles and double strand A, CO 22 (24, 26, 30, 32) sts. Work picot hem as for back, changing to larger needles after completion of first black stripe, and cont with stripe patt until piece measures 4¾ (5¼, 5½, 6, 6¾) in. above eyelet row, ending with a WS row.

Shape armhole: BO 4 sts beg next row, and cont as set until piece measures 7½ (8¼, 9, 10, 10½) in. from eyelet row, ending with a RS row.

Shape neck: BO 4 (4, 4, 5, 6) sts beg next row, then dec 1 st at neck edge beg every WS row 3 times, and then every fourth WS row 1 time to 10 (12, 14, 17, 18) sts. Work until piece measures the same as the back, and put sts onto a holder, leaving a long tail to k shoulder seam later.

Right front

Work as for left front, reversing the armhole and neck shaping.

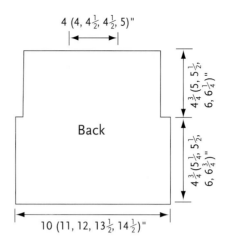

4 (4, 4½, 4½, 5)"

Back

4¾ (5, 5½, 6, 6¼)"

4¾ (5¼, 5½, 6, 6¾)"

10 (11, 12, 13½, 14½)"

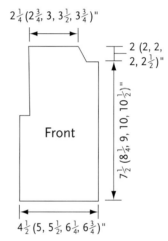

2¼ (2¾, 3, 3½, 3¾)"

2 (2, 2, 2, 2½)"

Front

7½ (8¼, 9, 10, 10½)"

4½ (5, 5½, 6¼, 6¾)"

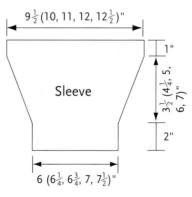

9½ (10, 11, 12, 12½)"

1"

Sleeve

3½ (4¼, 5, 6, 7)"

2"

6 (6¼, 6¾, 7, 7½)"

onto a size 7 dpn, and hold the two needles parallel to each other. Insert a third dpn into the first st on the first needle as if to k, then into the first st on the second needle as if to k, and k the 2 sts as one, using the double strand left from shoulder sts. Rep this a second time—there should now be 2 sts on the right needle. *Pass the first st on the right needle over the second and BO.* K the next set of sts on the parallel dpns tog, and rep from * to *. Cont in this way, knitting the corresponding sts of each shoulder tog and binding off as you go, until 1 st rem on the right needle. Break yarn, and pull through last st to secure. Rep this process for right shoulder.

Neckband: Beg at right front neck edge with RS facing, use size 5 circ needle and double strand A to pick up and k 18 (18, 18, 19, 22) sts up neck shaping to shoulder seam. K across 20 (20, 22, 22, 24) sts from the holder for the neck, and then pick up and k 18 (18, 18, 19, 22) sts down the left front to the neck edge—56 (56, 58, 60, 68) sts total. Beg with a p row, work seven rows st st.

Next row (RS)—work eyelet: K1, * k2tog, yo*; rep from * to * across, end k1.
Beg with a p row, work seven more rows st st. BO.

Button band

With smaller needle, double strand A, RSs facing, and starting at eyelet row of neckband at left front for girl and eyelet row of lower right front hem for boy, pick up and k 40 (44, 50, 56, 58) sts down to eyelet row of left front lower hem for girl and up to eyelet row of right front neckband for boy.
Beg with a p row, work nine rows st st.

Next row (RS)—work eyelet: K1, *k2tog, yo*; rep from * to * to end, end k1.
Beg with a p row, work nine more rows st st; BO.

Buttonhole band

Pick up sts as you did for button band, but on the opposite front.
Beg with a p row, and work three rows st st.

Next row (RS)—buttonhole row: K 3 (3, 3, 3, 4), BO 2, *k 6 (4, 5, 6, 6), BO 2*; rep from * to * 4 (6, 6, 6, 6) times, end k 3 (3, 3, 3, 4).

Sleeves

With size 5 needles and double strand A, CO 28 (30, 32, 34, 36) sts.

Make hem in st st: Work 2 rows A, [2 rows B, 2 rows A] 3 times (14 rows total).

Next row (RS): Still using A, work eyelet row—k1, *k2tog, yo*; rep from * to * across, end k1.
P one row.
Still using yarn A and small needles, work two more rows st st.
Change to B, and work four rows.
Beg stripe patt (four rows A, four rows B), and work eight rows more with small needles.
Change to larger needles and continuing with stripe patt as set, inc 1 st each end this RS row, then every RS row 6 (4, 5, 2, 1) times, and then every fourth row 2 (4, 5, 8, 10) times to 46 (48, 54, 56, 60) sts.
Cont without further shaping until the sleeve measures 6½ (7¼, 8, 9, 10) in. above eyelet row; BO.

Neckband

Before working neckband, the shoulders need to be joined. Use the BO seam technique for shoulder seams as follows: With RSs facing each other, place the sts from the left front and back shoulder each

Next row: P, and CO 2 sts over each buttonhole as follows: P 4 (4, 4, 4, 5), turn, CO 2, turn, *p 6 (4, 5, 6, 6), turn, CO 2, turn*; rep from * to * 4 (6, 6, 6, 6) times, end p2 (2, 2, 2, 3).
Work four more rows st st, and then work eyelet row as for button band.
Beg with a p row, work three rows st st; then work another buttonhole row for hem side as before.

Next row (WS): P, casting on 2 sts over bound-off sts as before.
Work four rows st st, binding off on last row.

Finishing

Weave in the loose ends. Lightly steam everything to block.

Match center of sleeve tops to shoulder seam with RSs facing each other, and pin in place. Backstitch sleeve top to armhole edge, sewing the bound-off sts at armhole edges to the straight side edges at the top of the sleeves. Lightly steam seams. Sew sleeve and side seams, including hem.
Turn all hems under, and lightly steam. Steam sleeve and side seams while you're at it. Pin hems (sleeves, bottom, button bands, and neckband) in place. Sew hems down. Steam again, if necessary. Work buttonhole st around buttonholes to join them. Sew buttons opposite buttonholes using a contrasting thread or yarn.

BUMBLEBEE HAT

With size 5 needles and double strand A, CO 76 (88, 96) sts. Work 8 rows st st.

Next row (RS)—work eyelet turning row: K1, *k2tog, yo*; rep from * to * across, end k1.
P one row.
Still using A, beg stripe patt (four rows A, four rows B), and work for 1½ (2¼, 3) in. above eyelet row, changing to larger needles upon completion of second stripe, ending with a WS row.

Beg shaping top: *Ssk, k 15 (18, 20), k2tog*; rep from * to * 3 times (dec 8 sts/row)—68 (80, 88) sts. Work three rows even.

Next row (RS): *Ssk, k 13 (16, 18), k2tog*; rep from * to * across—60 (72, 80) sts. Cont shap-

ing, decreasing 8 sts as set every fourth row 6 (8, 9) more times to 12 (8, 8) sts. Finish stripe.

Antennae: Put first 6 (4, 4) sts onto size 5 dpn, and put rem 6 (4, 4) sts onto holder.

Work I-cord: With double strand B, k across row with a second dpn. For the two larger sizes, work first row of I-cord as follows: K1, m1, k2, m1, k1— to end up with 6 sts. All sizes: *Slide the sts to the opposite end of the needle, and k them.* Rep from * to * for 3 in. Break yarn, pull ends down through center of cord to conceal. Rep process for second antenna.

Finishing: Weave in loose ends. Sew back seam, including hem. Turn hem to form picot edge, steam, and pin in place. Sew hem. Make two 1½-in. pom-poms in A, leaving a 10-in. tail. Use the tail to attach the pom-poms to the antennae, bring ends down through the center of the I-cord antennae, and secure. Tack antennae tog at their base with matching yarn, so they won't split apart too much.

COPYCAT

Over the past few years, I have had numerous
unfinished designs in my notebook that are half
black and half white. With this set, I finally committed
those ideas to yarn and needles. This unisex cotton jumpsuit
is knit in two separate halves and then sewn up the middle.
With simple Fair Isle details at the cuffs and on the pockets,
and easy-to-follow shaping instructions, it knits up quite
quickly. The matching hat is knit in one piece and sewn
up the back. Button bands along the inside
leg seams make diapering easy. Try changing the color
combination to some other opposites—blue and orange
would look terrific—or use wool instead of cotton
for a warmer winter set.

COPYCAT

Black and White Jumpsuit with Matching Hat

∴ MATERIALS

Jumpsuit

2 (2, 3, 3) 50g skeins each Tahki Cotton Classic (108 yd./skein) in black #3002 (A) and white #3001 (B), or other light worsted weight yarn that will knit to the gauge given below

Size 5 (3.75mm) knitting needles

Size 7 (4.5mm) knitting needles, or size needed to match gauge given below

24-in. size 5 circ knitting needle for leg button bands

One $\frac{7}{8}$-in. to 1-in. button to match A, and one $\frac{7}{8}$-in. to 1-in. button to match B for shoulder straps

6 (8, 8, 8) $\frac{1}{2}$-in. to $\frac{5}{8}$-in. buttons to match B for leg button band

Row counter, stitch markers, stitch holders, and tapestry needle

Hat

1 skein each A and B

1$\frac{1}{4}$-in. commercial pom-pom maker

Set

3 (3, 4, 4) skeins each A and B

∴ SIZES

Jumpsuit: 6 months (1, 2, 3 years)

Length (cuff to shoulder): 18$\frac{1}{2}$ (21$\frac{1}{2}$, 24, 27) in.

Chest: 18 (20, 22, 24) in.

Hat circumference: 16 (17$\frac{1}{2}$, 19) in.

∴ GAUGE

21 sts and 28 rows to 4 in. in st st on size 7 (4.5mm) needles

30 sts and 28 rows to 4 in. over color patts on size 5 (3.75mm) needles

Don't waste precious time and precious yarn—make a gauge swatch before beginning!

∴ PATTERN STITCHES

M1 right (right-slanting, make 1 inc): Insert left needle from back to front into the horizontal strand bet the last st k on the right needle and the first st on the left needle, and pick it up onto the left needle. K this lifted strand through the front.

M1 left (left-slanting, make 1 inc): Insert left needle from front to back into the horizontal strand bet the last st k on the right needle and the first st on the left needle, and pick it up onto the left needle. K this lifted strand through back of loop.

Sl2, k1, p2sso: Sl next 2 sts tog (at same time) as if to k. K the next st. Pass the 2 sl sts tog (at the same time) over the k st and off right needle.

JUMPSUIT

Right half

With size 5 needles and B, CO 47 (53, 57, 63) sts. K 2 rows.

Next row (RS): Beg row one of chart A where indicated on chart for size being knit, and work through last row of chart.
K three rows B.

Next row (RS): Change to A and larger needles, slip on row counter, and shape leg as follows:
K1, m1 right, k22 (25, 27, 30), m1 right, pm, k1 (center axis st), pm, m1 left, k22 (25, 27, 30), m1 left, k1—51 (57, 61, 67) sts.
Cont as established, increasing 1 st each end and 1 st each side of center axis st (4 sts total per inc row), slipping markers as you go, every 8th (10th, 12th, 14th) row 4 more times to 67 (73, 77, 83) sts. Work without further shaping, still slipping markers for axis st, until leg measures 7 (8, 9, 10) in. from beg, ending with a WS row.

Shape crotch: BO 3 sts beg next 2 rows; then dec 1 st (by ssk beg row and k2tog end of row) each end every RS row twice—57 (63, 67, 73) sts. Work last WS row even.

Shape hip: Reset row counter to zero. K across to within 2 sts of first axis st marker, ssk, sl marker, k1 (axis st), sl marker, k2tog, k to end.
Cont shaping hip as set every 8th (10th, 12th, 14th) row 4 more times to 47 (53, 57, 63) sts. Work without further shaping until piece measures 13½ (16, 18, 20) in. from beg, ending with a WS row.

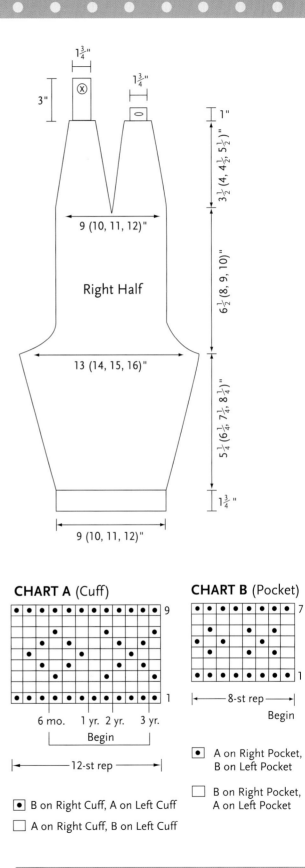

Right Half

1¾"

1¾"

3"

1"

3½ (4, 4½, 5½)"

9 (10, 11, 12)"

6½ (8, 9, 10)"

13 (14, 15, 16)"

5¼ (6¼, 7¼, 8¼)"

1¾"

9 (10, 11, 12)"

CHART A (Cuff)

9

1

6 mo. 1 yr. 2 yr. 3 yr.

Begin

|← 12-st rep →|

☐● B on Right Cuff, A on Left Cuff
☐ A on Right Cuff, B on Left Cuff

CHART B (Pocket)

7

1

|← 8-st rep →|

Begin

● A on Right Pocket, B on Left Pocket

☐ B on Right Pocket, A on Left Pocket

Divide for front and back bodice and armhole: K across first 22 (25, 27, 30) sts, k2tog, join second ball A, and k across rem 23 (26, 28, 31) sts for back bodice. You should now have 23 (26, 28, 31) sts each for front and back bodices.
Work and shape front and back bodices simultaneously using the two balls of yarn.

Next row (WS): P even.

Next row (RS): Dec 1 st each end of front bodice sts by ssk beg row, and k2tog end of row.

Rep for back bodice sts.

Cont shaping both bodices as established every RS row 2 (3, 3, 4) more times and then every fourth row 4 (4, 5, 6) times to 9 (10, 10, 9) sts each side.
Work without further shaping until piece measures 17 (20, 22½, 25½) in. from beg, ending with a WS row. Put the 9 (10, 10, 9) sts from front

onto size 5 needles. Put the 9 (10, 10, 9) sts for back onto holder.

Work buttonhole strap onto front sts as follows:

Row 1 (RS): K.

Row 2 (WS): K2, p5 (6, 6, 5), k2.
Rep these last two rows once more.

Next row—work buttonhole (RS): K4, yo, k2tog, k3 (4, 4, 3).

Next row (WS): Rep row two.
Rep rows one and two twice more, binding off on last row in patt.

Button strap: Put sts from back onto size 5 needle.

Row 1 (RS): K.

Row 2 (WS): K2, p5 (6, 6, 5), k2.
Rep these two rows for 3 in. BO in patt.

Left half

Work as for right half, only reverse colors, and work until you finish bodice shaping and are ready to work straps. Work straps as for right half, only reverse order—work button strap on first set of RS sts (back bodice), and then work buttonhole strap on last set of sts (front bodice).

Right pocket

With size 7 needles and B, CO 17 sts. First row will be WS—p this row.

Next row (RS): K1, m1 right, k across until 1 st rem, m1 left, k1.
Rep these last 2 rows once more—21 sts.
Work without further shaping until pocket measures 3 in., ending with a WS row. Change to A, and k two rows.

Next row (RS): Beg working chart B at row one. Complete chart through last row. K two more rows in A, binding off on last row.

Left pocket

Work as for right pocket, only reverse colors.

Finishing

Weave in loose ends on all pieces, and steam. Fold jumpsuit halves in half along outside leg and hip shaping, matching up crotch points and inside leg edges; lightly steam. Lay out left and right halves with the two fronts adjacent to each other, lining up crotch points and neck shaping. Sew crotch-to-neck seam.

Attach pockets: Attach right pocket to right half on front (the side with the buttonhole strap) so that the bottom edge of the pocket is lined up with the beg of the crotch shaping and so that the pocket is centered horizontally bet the hip shaping and the center front. Rep for left pocket. Sew crotch-to-neck seam on back.

Button band on inside leg: With RS facing and beg at bottom of cuff on back left leg, use size 5 circ needle and B to pick up and k 35 (42, 47, 52) sts up leg to crotch seam. Then pick up and k another 35 (42, 47, 52) sts down the other side to the bottom of the cuff on the right back leg—70 (84, 94, 104) sts total. K 2 rows.

Row 3 (WS): K2, p to last 2 sts, k2.

Row 4 (RS): K.

Row 5: Rep row three.
K two rows, binding off on last row.

Buttonhole band: Using yarn A, work as for button band, picking up 70 (84, 94, 104) sts from bottom of cuff on right front to bottom of cuff on left front and completing first 3 rows.

Row 4 (RS)—work buttonholes: K3 (4, 3, 4), *yo, k2tog, k11 (9, 11, 12)*; rep from * to * 1 (2, 2, 2) more time, yo, k2tog, k8 (6, 6, 8); rep from * to * 2 (3, 3, 3) times, yo, k2tog, end k3 (4, 3, 4). Finish from here (from row 5) as you did for button band. Weave in loose ends from button bands.
Sew smaller buttons opposite holes on leg button band using a few separated ply of yarn A, and button up. Take a strand of matching yarn in a tapestry needle, and tack the buttonhole band to the button band at the hem of the cuff to secure; make sure it overlaps neatly. Sew larger buttons onto shoulder straps using a few separated ply of yarn A for the B-colored button, and yarn B for the A-colored button.

HAT

With size 5 needles and A, CO 84 (92, 100) sts.
K 2 rows.

Next row (RS)—beg stripe patt: Without cutting A, change to B, and beg with a k row; work two rows st st, carrying yarn A up the side by twisting the two strands tog (to avoid having to weave in a lot of ends).
Change back to A (without cutting B), and work two rows st st. Rep last four rows once more, and work two more rows B in st st. K two rows A.

Next row (RS): Changing to larger needles and still using A, k across first 42 (46, 50) sts. Change to B, twisting yarns at back of work, and k across rem 42 (46, 50) sts.

Next row (WS): P across first 42 (46, 50) sts in B, switch to A—again, twisting yarns tog on WS of work to avoid gaps—and p across rem 42 (46, 50) sts.
Cont as established, working one-half A and one-half B, for 1 (1¼, 1½) in., or 3 (3¼, 3½) in. from beg, ending with a WS row.

Shape top: K across first 20 (22, 24) sts, sl2, k1, p2sso; k next 19 (21, 23) sts rem of A. Change to B, and k first 19 (21, 23) sts, sl2, k1, p2sso; k rem 20 (22, 24) sts—80 (88, 96) sts.
Work WS even, maintaining color blocks.

Next row (RS): K across first 19 (21, 23) sts, sl2, k1, p2sso; k rem 18 (20, 22) sts of A. Change to B, and k first 18 (20, 22) sts, sl2, k1, p2sso; k rem 19 (21, 23) sts—76 (84, 92) sts.
Work WS even.
Cont to dec 4 sts/row as established every RS row until 32 (36, 40) sts rem. BO purlwise.

Finishing

Weave in ends. Sew back seam. Lay hat flat, RSs out, with back seam centered. Sew top seam, using matching yarn for the two different-colored halves. Steam hat. Make two 1¼-in. pom-poms—one in A and one in B, leaving tails long enough to attach pom-poms to top corners of hat. Sew A-colored pom-pom to B-colored hat corner and B-colored pom-pom to A-colored hat corner.

STRIPE IT RICH

This is a classic vest that can be dressed up or down,
knit in wool or cotton, or worn by a boy or a girl.
Many knitters tell me they have made it for their children
and grandchildren to wear over the winter holidays.
It's also a good project for someone who wants to practice
two-handed color knitting without the distraction of a complex
color work pattern. A few people have asked me
why I didn't make it easy and just do the stripes as
a slip-stitch pattern, or knit the vest sideways, but I like
the denser fabric the two-color knitting creates. My sample
vest has been shipped to stores all over
the country as part of a trunk show and has hung in
knitting markets and yarn shops, yet it still holds its shape
and looks as neat and tidy as ever.

STRIPE IT RICH

Unisex Striped Wool Vest with Matching Beanie

Vest

2 (3, 4) 25g skeins Rowan Lightweight DK Wool (67m or 73 yd./skein) in black #62 (A), 1 (1, 2) skein each in blue #51 (B), yellow #14 (C), and green #431 (D), and 1 skein in red #44 (E), or yarn that will knit to the gauge given below
Three ¾-in. buttons
Size 5 (3.75mm) knitting needles, or size needed to match gauge given below
Set of size 5 (3.75mm) dpns
Size 5 circ needle for edgings
Tapestry needle and stitch holders

Beanie

Two skeins A, one skein each B, C, D, and E—all sizes
Size 5 (3.75mm) knitting needles, or size needed to match gauge given below
Two size 5 (3.75mm) dpns

∴ SIZES

6–9 months (1–2, 3–4 years)
Length: 9½ (11½, 13½) in.
Chest: 21½ (25½, 29) in.
Hat circumference: S-15½ (M-17, L-18½, XL-20) in.

∴ GAUGE

30 sts and 28 rows to 4 in./10cm over stripe pattern on size 5 needles
24 sts and 28 rows to 4 in. over plain st st on size 5 needles
Don't waste precious time and precious yarn—make a gauge swatch before beginning!

∴ PATTERN STITCH

Vertical stripe pattern (in st st)

Row 1 (RS): *K2 A, k2 B, C, or D (see note)*; rep from * to * across row to last 2 sts, and k2 A.

Row 2 (WS): *P2 A, p2 B, C, or D*; rep from * to * across row to last 2 sts, and p2 A.

Note: The back is worked in A and B, the right front in A and C, and the left front in A and D.

VEST

Back

With size 5 needles and A, CO 78 (94, 110) sts.

Row 1: Work first row of stripe pattern using A and B.

Row 2: Work second row of stripe patt. Cont working with patt as established until back measures 5 (6, 7) in.

Shape armhole: BO 5 sts beg next 2 rows. BO 2 sts beg next 6 rows. Dec 1 st each end next 2 (3, 3) rows to 52 (66, 82) sts. Cont working in patt until armhole measures 4½ (5½, 6½) in., ending with a WS row.

Shape neck: Patt 12 (18, 22), BO center 28 (30, 38) sts in patt; patt rem 12 (18, 22) sts. Put both sets of shoulder sts onto holders for later.

Right front

With size 5 needles and A, CO 42 (50, 54) sts.

Row 1: Begin first row of stripe patt using A and C.

Row 2: Work second row of stripe patt. Cont working with patt as established until piece measures 5 (6, 7) in., ending with RS row.

Shape armhole and neck at the same time: For armhole, BO 5 sts beg this WS row, then 2 sts beg every WS row 3 times, and then 1 st beg every WS row 2 (3, 3) times. For the neck, dec 1 st beg every RS row 17 (18, 18) times to 12 (18, 22) sts. Work until right front measures the same as the back, and leave rem sts on a holder for later.

Left front

Using A and D, work left front as for right front, but reverse armhole shaping to RS and neck shaping to WS.

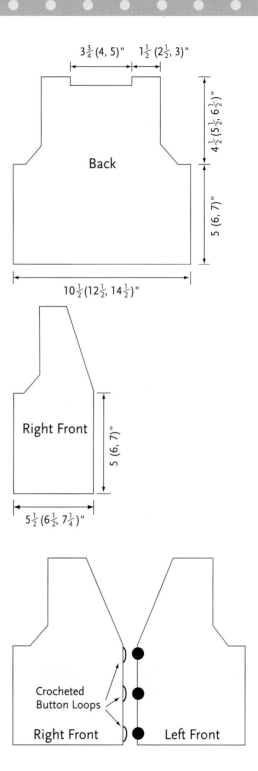

3¾ (4, 5)"   1½ (2½, 3)"

Back

4½ (5½, 6½)"

5 (6, 7)"

10½ (12½, 14½)"

Right Front

5 (6, 7)"

5½ (6½, 7¼)"

Crocheted Button Loops

Right Front

Left Front

Finishing

Weave in loose ends.

Join shoulders: Use the BO seam technique for shoulder seams as follows: With RSs facing each other, place the sts from the left front and back shoulder each onto a size 5 dpn, and hold the two needles parallel to each other. Insert a third dpn into the first st on the first needle as if to k, then into the first st on the second needle as if to k, and using yarn A, k the 2 sts as one. Rep this a second time—there should now be 2 sts on the right needle. *Pass the first st on the right needle over the second, and BO.* K the next set of sts on the dpns tog, and rep from * to *. Cont in this way, knitting the corresponding sts of each shoulder tog and binding off as you go, until 1 st rem on the right needle. Break the yarn, and pull through last st to secure. Rep this process for the

tip

If you don't know how to do two-handed color knitting, this project is a good one to practice on. For instructions on this technique, also known as Fair Isle or stranded knitting, see Alice Starmore's *Book of Fair Isle Knitting*, The Taunton Press, 1993.

right shoulder. (For more on knitted seams, see *Knitting Tips & Trade Secrets*, The Taunton Press, 1996, p. 107.) Lightly steam shoulder seams and the vest pieces to block.

Armhole edging: With RSs facing, use size 5 circ needle and E (red) to pick up and k 36 (44, 52) sts up left front armhole, 1 st at shoulder seam, and 36 (44, 52) sts down left back armhole—73 (89, 105) sts. K 1 WS row.

Next row: BO all sts knitwise. Backstitch side seams tog.

Front and neck edging: With RS facing and starting at right front bottom corner, use size 5 circ needle and E to pick up and k 33 (39, 45) sts up straight front edge, 33 (39, 45) sts up neck to shoulder seam, 25 (27, 32) sts across back neck, 33 (39, 45) sts down left front neck, and 33 (39, 45) sts down left front straight edge—157 (183, 212) sts. K 1 WS row.

Next row: BO all sts knitwise.

Hem edging: With RS facing and starting at lower left front edge, use size 5 circ needle and E to pick up and k 2 sts from bottom of left front edging, 36 (43, 48) sts across lower left front to side seam, 69 (81, 94) sts across lower back edge, 36 (43, 48) sts across lower right front, and 2 sts from bottom of right front red edging—145 (171, 194) sts. K 1 WS row.

Next row: BO all sts knitwise. Lightly steam press vest, side seams, and edgings to neaten.

Button loops: These button loops are not loops per se, in that they lie flush with the edging and are nearly invisible. This is to ensure that the vest

front looks symmetrical when buttoned. Starting from the bottom right front, use a crochet hook and E to sl st for ½ in. from bottom. *Chain st for ¾ in. for button loop, rejoin ¾ in. from where you left off, and sl st for 1 (1½, 2) in.* Rep from * to * once. Chain st for ¾ in. for third loop, rejoin ¾ in. from where you left off, and sl st to beg neck shaping. Break yarn, and pull through last st. Weave in ends. Sew buttons to the edge of the red trim on the left front opposite loops, as shown on p. 101.

BEANIE

With size 5 needles and E, CO 93 (102, 111, 120) sts.

Row 1 (RS): P.

Row 2: K.

Changing to A and beg on RS with a k row, work st st in the following horizontal stripe patt: Two rows A, two rows B, two rows A, two rows C, two rows A, two rows D, two rows A. Changing back to E and beg with a RS row, k two rows.

Next row (RS): P.

Changing back to A and beg with a p row, work st st for 1½ (1¾, 2, 2¾) in. above last red stripe, ending with a WS row.

Shape crown—row 1: *K4, k2tog*; rep from * to * across row, ending k3 (0, 3, 0)—78 (85, 93, 100) sts.

Row 2: P.

Row 3: As for row 1, only end k0 (1, 3, 4)—65 (71, 78, 84) sts.

Row 4: P.

Row 5: *K2, k2tog across row, ending k1 (3, 2, 0)—49 (54, 59, 63) sts.

Row 6: P.

Row 7: As for row 5, only end k1 (2, 3, 3)—37 (41, 45, 48) sts.

Row 8: P.

Row 9: As for row 5, only end k1 (1, 1, 0)—28 (31, 34, 36) sts.

Row 10: P.

Row 11: *K1, k2tog*; rep from * to * across row, ending k1 (1, 1, 0)—19 (21, 23, 24) sts.

Row 12: P.

Row 13: K2tog across row, ending k1 (1, 1, 0)—10 (11, 12, 12) sts.

Row 14: P2tog across row, ending p0 (1, 0, 0)—5 (6, 6, 6) sts.

I-cord top loop: Break yarn, and attach B (blue). Put the 5 (6, 6, 6) rem sts onto a size 5 dpn. K across row with a second dpn. *Slide the sts to the opposite end of the needle, and k them.* Rep from * to * for 4 in. Break yarn, leaving a 10-in. tail, pull through sts, and secure. Weave in loose ends. Lightly steam press the striped area to prevent curling, and sew back seam. Pull top of I-cord down into a loop, and sew end to base of I-cord at top of hat.

MOOD INDIGO

This vest, hat, and pants set is knit in real indigo
dyed cotton, a yarn that shrinks, fades, and wears
like denim. It actually improves with washing and drying
in the dryer. The only drawback is that you have to knit the
garment a few inches longer than the actual final size,
which some people are fundamentally opposed to,
and your fingers turn blue while you're knitting with it.
But look at it this way—you don't have to block,
hand-wash, or air-dry, so you may actually be saving time
in the long run. If you still don't want to use the denim yarn,
instructions and measurements for nonshrinking yarn are
included. This set, in a garter-stitch and stockinette-stitch
stripe pattern, is very easy and has minimal finishing.

MOOD INDIGO

Unisex Garter-Striped Denim Vest, Pants, and Hat

❖ MATERIALS

Vest

3 (3, 3, 4, 5, 5) 50g balls Rowan Denim or Elann indigo-dyed cotton (93m/ball), or other worsted weight yarn that will knit to the gauge given below
Size 7 (4.5mm) knitting needles, or size needed to match gauge given below
Size 5 (3.75mm) knitting needles
Set of size 7 (4.5mm) dpns for shoulder seams
Tapestry needle, stitch holders
Five ½-in. to ⅝-in. machine-washable buttons

Pants

6 (7, 8) balls denim
1 yd. elastic for waistband

Hat

2 (2, 2) balls denim
Crochet hook for tie

Set

Vest, pants, and hat, 1–3 years: 10 (12, 13) balls denim
Vest and hat, all sizes: 4 (5, 5, 6, 6, 7) balls

❖ SIZES

Vest: 6–9 months (1, 2, 3, 4, 6 years)
Length (after wash): 10 (11, 12, 12½, 13½, 15) in.
Chest: 20 (22, 24, 26, 28, 30) in.
Pants: 1 (2, 3) year
Length (after wash): 14 (16, 18) in.
Hat circumference: S-15 (M-17, L-18½) in.

❖ GAUGE (BEFORE WASH)

20 sts and 28 rows to 4 in./10cm over st st on size 7 (4.5mm) needles
After wash: 20 sts and 32 rows to 4 in./10cm
Don't waste precious time and precious yarn—make a gauge swatch before beginning!

❖ PATTERN STITCH

Garter-stitch stripe pattern: Six rows st st, eight rows (four ridges) g st

VEST

Back

With size 5 needles, CO 50 (54, 60, 65, 70, 75) sts.
Work 8 rows g st (k every row).
Change to larger needles, and work stripe patt (6 rows st st, 8 rows g st) for 6½ (7¼, 7¾, 8½, 9, 10¼) in. [5½ (6, 6½, 7, 7½, 8½) in.], ending with a WS row.

Shape armhole: BO 3 sts beg next 2 rows; then dec 1 st each end every RS row (by ssk at the beg of the row, and k2tog at the end of the row) 5 times to 34 (38, 44, 49, 54, 59) sts. Cont without further shaping until armhole measures 5½ (6, 6½, 6½, 7¼, 7¾) in. [4½ (5, 5½, 5½, 6, 6½) in.], ending 1 row short of a full-, half-, quarter-, or three-quarter stripe. Work across 8 (9, 11, 13, 15, 17) sts, and put onto holder. BO center 18 (20, 22, 23, 24, 25) sts for back neck, work across rem 8 (9, 11, 13, 15, 17) sts, and put onto holder for later.

Right front

With size 5 needles, CO 27 (30, 32, 35, 37, 40) sts.
Work 8 rows g st.

Change to larger needles, and work stripe patt for 6½ (7¼, 7¾, 8½, 9, 10¼) in. [5½ (6, 6½, 7, 7½, 8½) in.], ending with a RS row.

Shape armhole: BO 3 sts beg this WS row.
Now shape neck and remainder of armhole at the same time. Dec 1 st by ssk beg every RS row (neck edge) 11 (13, 13, 14, 14, 15) times; dec 1 st by k2tog at end of every RS row (armhole edge) 5 times—ending up with 8 (9, 11, 13, 15, 17) sts. Cont without further shaping until piece measures same as back, and put sts on holder, leaving a 20-in. tail to k shoulders tog later. Place markers for buttonholes ½ in. up from hem, ½ in. down from beg neck shaping, and 3 more markers evenly spaced bet (5 total).

Left front

Work as for right front, only work buttonholes opposite markers on RS rows as follows: Knit to last 4 sts,

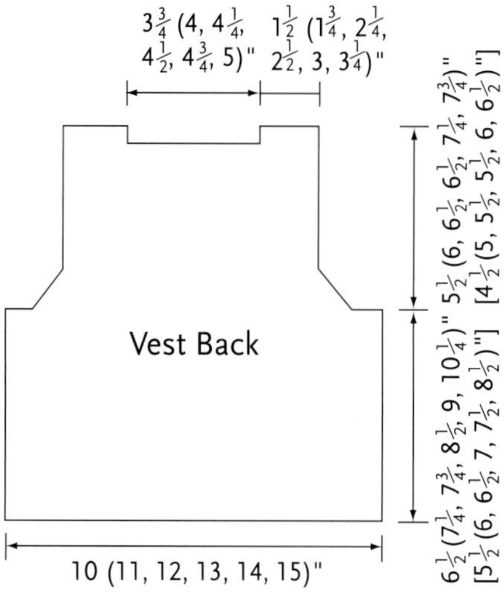
3¾ (4, 4¼, 4½, 4¾, 5)"
1½ (1¾, 2¼, 2½, 3, 3¼)"
Vest Back
10 (11, 12, 13, 14, 15)"
6½ (7¼, 7¾, 8½, 9, 10¼)" 5½ (6, 6½, 6½, 7¼, 7¾)"
[5½ (6, 6½, 7, 7½, 8½)"] [4½ (5, 5½, 5½, 6, 6½)"]

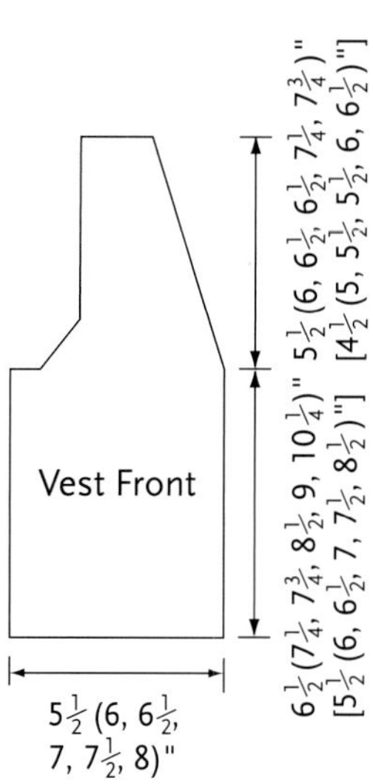
Vest Front
5½ (6, 6½, 7, 7½, 8)"
6½ (7¼, 7¾, 8½, 9, 10¼)" 5½ (6, 6½, 6½, 7¼, 7¾)"
[5½ (6, 6½, 7, 7½, 8½)"] [4½ (5, 5½, 5½, 6, 6½)"]

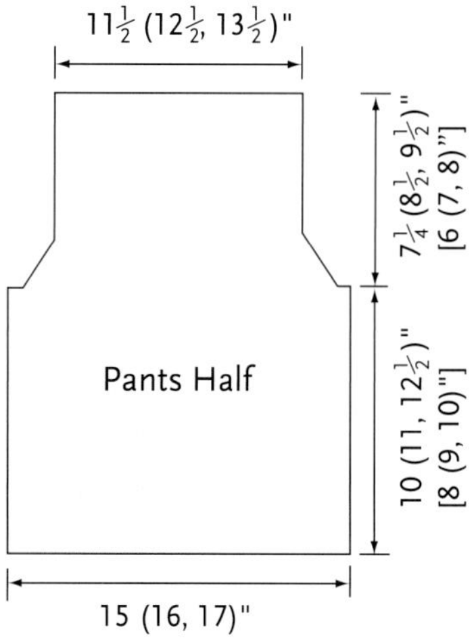
11½ (12½, 13½)"
7¼ (8½, 9½)"
[6 (7, 8)"]
Pants Half
10 (11, 12½)"
[8 (9, 10)"]
15 (16, 17)"

yo, k2tog, k2. Work to 6½ (7¼, 7¾, 8½, 9, 10¼) in. [5½ (6, 6½, 7, 7½, 8½) in.], ending with a WS row.

Shape armhole and neck (RS): BO 3 sts beg this row, and k2tog at end of row for neck. Work WS even. Dec 1 st by ssk at armhole every RS row 5 times, and 1 st at neck edge by k2tog at end of every RS row 10 (12, 12, 13, 13, 14) more times to 8 (9, 11, 13, 15, 17) sts. Work until left front measures same as back.

Finishing

Use the BO seam technique for shoulder seams as follows: With RSs facing each other, place the sts from the left front and back shoulder each onto a size 7 dpn, and hold the two needles parallel to each other. Insert a third dpn into the first st on the first needle as if to k, then into the first st on the second needle as if to k, and k the 2 sts as one. Rep this a second time—there should now be 2 sts on the right needle. *Pass the first st on the right needle over the second, and BO.* K the next set of sts on the dpns tog, and rep from * to *. Cont in this way, knitting

tip

Denim yarn shrinks in length by about 20% during the first wash/dry. Allowances have been made for shrinkage in the instructions. However, if you would like to substitute a nonshrinking cotton or wool, follow the second set of measurements that appear in brackets in the instructions. These are the after-wash measurements. The hat instructions are the same for all yarns.

the corresponding sts of each shoulder tog and binding off as you go, until 1 st remains on the right needle. Cut yarn, pull through last st to secure. Rep this process for right shoulder. (For more on knitted seams, see *Knitting Tips & Trade Secrets*, The Taunton Press, 1996, p. 107.) Weave in loose ends.

If you used the denim yarn, wash and dry the pieces as instructed on ball band at this point. Otherwise, steam or block pieces and shoulder seams. Sew side seams. Sew buttons opposite the buttonholes.

PANTS

Left half

With size 5 needles, CO 75 (80, 85) sts. Work
8 rows g st.

Change to larger needles, and work stripe patt
(6 rows st st, 8 rows g st) for 10 (11, 12½) in.
[8 (9, 10) in.], ending with a WS row.

Shape crotch: BO 4 sts beg next 2 rows, and then
dec 1 st each end every RS row (by ssk at the beg
of the row, and k2tog at the end) 5 times to
57 (62, 67) sts. Cont without further shaping
until piece measures 15 (17¼, 19¾) in. [12 (14, 16)
in.] from beg, ending with a completed stripe.
Work another 2¼ in. [2 in.] in st st only, ending
with a WS row.

P next 2 rows for turning waistband. Change to
smaller needles.

Next row (RS): Beg with a k row, work 2¼ in.
[2 in.] more in st st. BO all sts.

Right half

Make identical to left half.

Finishing

Weave in loose ends. If using denim, wash and dry
according to ball band instructions. Sew front and
back crotch-to-waist seams, including waistband.
Sew inside leg seams, taking care to match garter
stripes. Steam crotch-to-waist seams and inside leg
seams, too. Fold over waistband hem to inside at
ridge, lightly steam and pin in place. Whipstitch
waistband around, leaving a 2-in. opening at center
back. Thread elastic through waistband, cut to
desired length (an inch or two shorter than the
child's waist should do it), and sew ends tog.
Whipstitch opening closed.

HAT

With size 5 needles, CO 75 (85, 92) sts. Work
8 rows g st.

Change to larger needles, and work stripe patt
(6 rows st st, 8 rows g st) for 6 (6, 8) stripes.
Work first two rows of next stripe (which should
be a st st stripe).

Work eyelet row (RS): *K3 (3, 2), k2tog, yo*; rep
from * to * across, ending k5 (5, 4). Finish this
st st stripe, and then work 16 rows g st, binding
off sts on last row.

Finishing: Weave in loose ends. If using denim,
wash and dry as instructed on ball band. Fold
piece in half lengthwise, and sew back seam.

Make tie: With crochet hook, make a 20-in. chain.
Thread chain in and out of eyelets, and pull tog
to cinch. Tie in a bow.

SNOW SUIT

Knitting this dressy little outfit fulfilled my then-unrequited
childhood desire for a muff. My favorite book as an
elementary school child was *The Wolves of Willoughby Chase*
by Joan Aiken, and this outfit looks to me like something
the two 19th-century heroines, Bonnie and Sylvia,
would have worn. A couple of knitters have written
to tell me that they lined the coat, making it even warmer.
I don't know how to make a lining, but if I were to knit
the coat again, I think I might consult a tailor about a lining.
This outfit goes so quickly that it can be knit in less than
a week. And by all means, don't omit the muff!
Your granddaughter will thank you later.

SNOW SUIT

Mohair-Trimmed Trapeze Jacket with Matching Beret and Muff

Jacket

3 (3, 4, 5) 100g skeins Classic Elite Montera (wool and llama blend, 127 yd./skein) in blue #093 (A) and 2 (2, 2, 3) 1½-oz. skeins Classic Elite La Gran Mohair (90 yd./skein) in white #6501 (B), or yarns that will knit to the gauge given below
Three large (size 4) sew-on snaps
Size 9 (5.5mm) knitting needles, or size needed to match gauge given below
Set of size 9 dpns for shoulder seams
Tapestry needle and stitch holders
Cardboard rectangles for pom-poms

Beret

1 skein each A and B
Size 8 (5mm) and size 9 (5.5mm) knitting needles

Muff

1 skein each A and B
Size 9 needles
Large crochet hook to chain st cord

Set

5 (5, 6, 6) skeins A, 3 skeins B

:• SIZES

2 (3, 4, 6) years
Length: 12½ (14, 15½, 17½) in.
Chest: 19 (21, 23, 25) in.
Sleeve: 10½ (11¼, 12, 13) in.
Beret: One size fits all

:• GAUGE

Both yarns: 16 sts and 20 rows to 4 in./10cm over st st on size 9 needles
Don't waste precious time and precious yarn—make a gauge swatch before beginning!

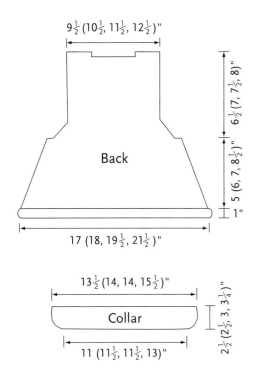

$9\frac{1}{2}$ $(10\frac{1}{2}, 11\frac{1}{2}, 12\frac{1}{2})$"

$6\frac{1}{2}$ $(7, 7\frac{1}{2}, 8)$"

Back

5 $(6, 7, 8\frac{1}{2})$"

1"

17 $(18, 19\frac{1}{2}, 21\frac{1}{2})$"

$13\frac{1}{2}$ $(14, 14, 15\frac{1}{2})$"

Collar

$2\frac{1}{2}$ $(2\frac{1}{2}, 3, 3\frac{1}{4})$"

11 $(11\frac{1}{2}, 11\frac{1}{2}, 13)$"

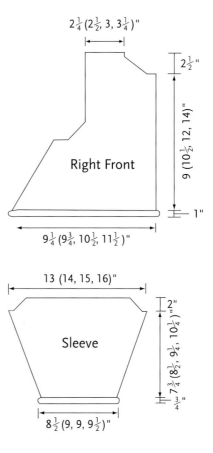

$2\frac{1}{4}$ $(2\frac{1}{2}, 3, 3\frac{1}{4})$"

$2\frac{1}{2}$"

Right Front

9 $(10\frac{1}{2}, 12, 14)$"

1"

$9\frac{1}{4}$ $(9\frac{3}{4}, 10\frac{1}{2}, 11\frac{1}{2})$"

13 (14, 15, 16)"

2"

Sleeve

$7\frac{3}{4}$ $(8\frac{1}{2}, 9\frac{1}{4}, 10\frac{1}{4})$"

$\frac{3}{4}$"

$8\frac{1}{2}$ $(9, 9, 9\frac{1}{2})$"

JACKET

Back

Using size 9 needles and B, CO 76 (82, 90, 100) sts. Work in st st for 2 in., ending with WS row, and decreasing 8 (10, 12, 14) sts evenly across last row to 68 (72, 78, 86) sts. Change to A. Work in st st, and dec 1 st each end every fifth row 6 (6, 7, 9) times to 56 (60, 64, 68) sts. Work until piece measures 5 (6, 7, 8½) in. from beg A, ending with a WS row.

> **Armhole shaping:** BO 4 sts beg next 2 rows; then dec 1 st each end every RS row 5 times to 38 (42, 46, 50) sts. Work until armhole measures 6½ (7, 7½, 8) in.

> **Next row:** Work 9 (10, 12, 13) sts, and put onto holder for later. BO center 20 (22, 22, 24) sts for back neck, work rem 9 (10, 12, 13) sts, and put onto holder for later.

Left front

With size 9 needles and B, CO 43 (46, 50, 54) sts. Work in st st for 2 in., ending with a WS row, and decreasing 6 (7, 8, 8) sts evenly across last row to

37 (39, 42, 46) sts. Change to A. Beg with a k row, work st st, decreasing 1 st beg every fifth row 6 (6, 7, 9) times to 31 (33, 35, 37) sts. Work until piece measures 5 (6, 7, 8½) in. from beg A, ending with a WS row.

> **Shape armhole:** BO 4 sts first row, and then dec 1 st beg every RS row 5 times to 22 (24, 26, 28) sts. Work without further shaping until piece measures 9 (10½, 12, 14) in. from beg A, ending with a RS row.

> **Shape neck:** BO 7 (7, 7, 8) sts beg next row (neck edge), and work to end. Work 1 row even. BO 3 sts beg next row. Work 1 row even. Now dec 1 st beg every WS row 3 (4, 4, 4) times to 9 (10, 12, 13) sts. Work until piece measures the same as the back, putting the rem 9 (10, 12, 13) sts onto a holder and leaving a 20-in. tail of yarn to k shoulder seam tog later.

to 54 (56, 56, 62) sts. Work collar without further shaping until it measures 2½ (2½, 3, 3¼) in. from beg; BO.

Finishing
Weave in loose ends. Lightly steam pieces, excluding mohair trim and collar.

Shoulder seams: Use the BO seam technique for shoulder seams as follows: With RSs facing each other, place the sts from the left front and back shoulder each onto a size 9 dpn, and hold the two needles parallel to each other. Insert a third dpn into the first st on the first needle as if to k, then into the first st on the second needle as if to k, and k the 2 sts as one. Rep this a second time—there should now be 2 sts on the right needle. *Pass the first st on the right needle over the second, and BO.* K the next set of sts on the parallel dpns tog, and rep from * to *. Cont in this way, knitting the corresponding sts of each shoulder tog and binding off as you go, until 1 st rem on the right needle. Break yarn, and pull through last st to secure. Rep this process for the right shoulder. Lightly steam shoulder seams.

Attach sleeves and collar: With RSs facing each other, pin sleeve caps to armholes, matching up bound-off sts of sleeve to bound-off sts of armhole. Backstitch in place. Sew inside sleeve seams and side seams, reversing seams for rolled mohair trim. With RS collar facing WS of jacket, center collar at back neck, and pin around. (The edges of the collar do not meet the neck edges.) Stitch collar in place, and turn back when finished. Lightly steam seams, avoiding mohair.

Pom-poms: Make three pom-poms as described on the facing page. Sew one pom-pom to right front neck edge. Sew second pom-pom ½ (1, 1½, 2) in. up from where mohair trim meets A on right front, and sew third pom-pom centered bet the first and second.

Snaps: Sew the top part of the snaps to the WS of right front under pom-poms, ½ in. in from edge. Sew bottom of snaps opposite these on RS of left front.

Right front
Work as for left front, reversing side, armhole, and neck shaping.

Sleeves
With size 9 needles and B, CO 40 (42, 42, 45) sts. Work in st st for 1½ in., ending with a WS row and decreasing 6 (6, 6, 7) sts evenly across last row to 34 (36, 36, 38) sts. Changing to A and beg with a k row, work 2 rows st st. Inc 1 st each end next row, then every other row 1 (0, 3, 3) time, and then every fourth row 7 (9, 8, 9) times to 52 (56, 60, 64) sts. Work until sleeve measures 7¾ (8½, 9¼, 10¼) in. from beg A.

Shape cap: BO 4 sts beg next 2 rows, and then dec 1 st each end every RS row 5 times to 34 (38, 42, 46) sts. Work 1 row even, then BO all sts.

Collar
The collar is worked entirely in yarn B in g st (k every row). With size 9 needles and B, CO 44 (46, 46, 52) sts. K 1 row.

Next row (inc): K1, m1, k across row until 1 st rem, m1, k1—46 (48, 48, 54) sts.
Rep this inc row next 2 rows to 50 (52, 52, 58) sts, and then rep same inc row every other row twice

BERET

With size 8 needle and A, CO 72 sts. Work in g st for 1½ in., ending with a WS row. Change to size 9 needles.

Next row (RS): *K1, k2 into next st*; rep from * to * across row to 108 sts.
Work st st for 4½ in., ending with a WS row.

Next row: *K2, k2tog; rep from * to end of row—81 sts.
Work three rows even.

Next row: *K2, k2tog; rep from * across, end k1—61 sts.
Work three rows even.

Next row: K1, *k2tog, k1; rep from * to end of row—41 sts.
P one row.

Next row: *K1, k2tog; rep from * across, end k2—28 sts.
P one row.

Next row: K2tog across—14 sts.
Rep last two rows once more to 7 sts. Break yarn, leaving a long enough tail to sew back seam. Pull through rem sts, and tighten.

Finishing: Weave in loose ends. Sew back seam. Make one pom-pom as instructed at right, only use a larger 1- to 1½-in. cardboard rectangle. Sew pom-pom to top center of beret.

MUFF (ONE SIZE)

With size 9 needles and B, CO 45 sts. Work in st st for 4 in., ending with a WS row. *P the next (RS) row, and k the following (WS) row*. Rep from * to * twice. Changing to A and beg with a k row (RS), work in st st until piece measures 7 in. from beg A, ending with a WS row.
Change back to B, and k one row.
K the next (WS) row, and p the following (RS) row. Rep from * to * twice.
Beg with a p row (WS), work in st st until piece measures 5 in. from end of A section; BO.

Pom-Poms

Wrap mohair around a ¾-in. to 1-in. cardboard rectangle 50 times. Take a 20-in. length of mohair, threaded into a tapestry needle, and pull it through the bottom edge of the form and the wrapped strands. Tie in a tight knot to secure, leaving ends to sew pom-pom to coat. Insert scissors into the top edge bet the form and the wrapped strands, and cut strands to free the pom-pom. If you need to make the pom-pom rounder and smaller, pull the pom-pom through a ring until the ring is wrapped around the pom-pom. Trim ends with scissors to desired size, remove ring, and re-fluff.

Finishing: Lightly steam blue section of knitted piece. With RSs facing each other, fold piece in half lengthwise, and sew top edges tog. Leaving the piece inside out, roll the mohair panels at each end back so that the cast-on edge and the bound-off edge touch. Whipstitch the two edges tog all the way around the center. Turn the piece RS out so that blue is on the outside, with rev st st mohair trim at edges on the sides.

Neck strap: Cut 3 strands of A six times longer than you want the strap to be. Hold the strands tog, and chain st to end to make strap. (You can use a crochet hook or simply chain st by hand.) Sew ends to top of muff at corners where A meets B. Make a pom-pom the same size as for jacket, and sew to center front of muff.

CLASSIC CABLES

I like oversized, beefy-looking cables and bobbles,
and the Hollow Oak cable seemed like a good choice for this
chunky yarn. This sweater, the first Monkeysuit to extend
to adult sizes, was intended as a classic Aran-style pullover
that would appeal to all ages and both genders. I also wanted
it to be simple enough for those trying their hand at cables
for the first time. (I remember knitting my first complicated cable
knit sweater—I had to place markers all the way across
the row to keep track of which cable was which.) I used a
second color for the cast-on edges because I don't like
to work in only one color, but you could certainly eliminate
that element if you don't feel like buying an extra skein of yarn.

CLASSIC CABLES

Unisex Cable Knit Pullover

MATERIALS

Pullover

4 (4, 6, 7, 8, 9, 11, 12, 14, 15) 100g skeins Classic Elite Artisan Wool/Alpaca (127 yd./116m per skein) in natural #016 (MC) and a small amount in blue #057 (CC) for edging, or chunky yarn that will knit to the gauge given below

Pair each of size 8 (5mm) and size 10 (6mm) knitting needles, or size needed to match gauge given below

Cable needle, 3 size 10 dpns for shoulder seams

Tapestry needle, stitch holders, row counter, markers

SIZES

Children: 1 (3, 5, 7, 9, 12) year; adult unisex: (S, M, L, XL)

Length: 13 (14, 16¼, 18¼, 19½, 21½, 23½, 24¾, 26¾, 28) in.

Chest: 28 (30, 35, 36½, 39, 41½, 45½, 50, 52½, 54½) in.

Sleeve: 1–12 years: 9 (10, 11, 12, 13, 14¼) in.; women's S–XL: 15½ (16, 16½, 17) in.; men's S–XL: 17 (17½, 18, 18½) in.

GAUGE

14 sts and 24½ rows to 4 in./10cm over seed st on size 10 needles; 25-stitch central cable panel on small sizes of pullover 4¼ in.; 37-stitch central cable panel on larger pullovers 6¼ in.

Don't waste precious time and precious yarn—make a gauge swatch before beginning!

PATTERN STITCHES

Seed st on an even number of sts.

> **Row 1:** *K1, p1; rep from * to end.

> **Row 2:** *P1, k1; rep from * to end.

Seed st on an odd number of sts.

> **All rows:** K1, *p1, k1; rep from * to end.

Make bobble: K into front, back, front, back, and front (5) of st. Then, without turning, bring fourth st over fifth and off, third st over fifth and off, second st

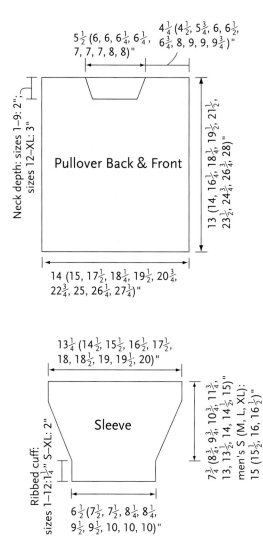

Neck depth: sizes 1–9: 2"; sizes 12–XL: 3"

5½ (6, 6, 6¼, 6¼, 7, 7, 7, 8, 8)"

4¼ (4½, 5¾, 6, 6½, 6¾, 8, 9, 9, 9¾)"

Pullover Back & Front

13 (14, 16¼, 18¼, 19½, 21½, 23½, 24¾, 26¾, 28)"

14 (15, 17½, 18¼, 19½, 20¾, 22¾, 25, 26¼, 27¼)"

13¼ (14½, 15½, 16½, 17½, 18, 18½, 19, 19½, 20)"

Sleeve

7¾ (8¾, 9¾, 10¾, 11¾, 13, 13½, 14, 14½, 15)" men's S (M, L, XL): 15 (15½, 16, 16½)"

Ribbed cuff: sizes 1–12: 1¼" S–XL: 2"

6½ (7½, 7½, 8¼, 8¼, 9½, 9½, 10, 10, 10)"

over fifth and off, and first over fifth and off—all in the same row.

Twist 3 back (t3b): Sl next st to cn, and hold at back of work, k2, p1 from cn.

Twist 3 front (t3f): Sl next 2 sts to cn, and hold at front of work, p1, k2 from cn.

Cable 4 front (c4f): Sl 2 sts to cn, and hold at front of work, k2, k2 from cn.

Cable panel A (over 6 sts)

Row 1 (RS): P1, k4, p1.

Row 2: K1, p4, k1.

Row 3: P1, c4f, p1.

Row 4: K1, p4, k1.
Rep these 4 rows for cable panel A.

Cable panel B (over 13 sts)

Row 1 (RS): P4, k2, make bobble, k2, p4.

Rows 2, 4, and 6: K4, p5, k4.

Row 3: P4, make bobble, k3, make bobble, p4.

Row 5: Rep row 1.

Row 7: P3, t3b, p1, t3f, p3.

Row 8: K3, p2, k1, p1, k1, p2, k3.

Row 9: P2, t3b, k1, p1, k1, t3f, p2.

Row 10: K2, p3, k1, p1, k1, p3, k2.

Row 11: P1, t3b, [p1, k1] twice, p1, t3f, p1.

Row 12: K1, p2, [k1, p1] 3 times, k1, p2, k1.

Row 13: P1, k3, [p1, k1] twice, p1, k3, p1.

Rows 14, 16, and 18: Rep rows 12, 10, and 8, respectively.

Row 15: P1, t3f, [p1, k1] twice, p1, t3b, p1.

Row 17: P2, t3f, k1, p1, k1, t3b, p2.

Row 19: P3, t3f, p1, t3b, p3.

Row 20: As for row 2.
Rep rows 1 to 20 for cable panel B.

PULLOVER

Back

With size 10 needles and CC, use the cable CO method or the 2-finger long-tail method to CO 59 (63, 71, 79, 83, 87, 95, 103, 107, 111) sts. Change to MC, and p first row, which is WS.

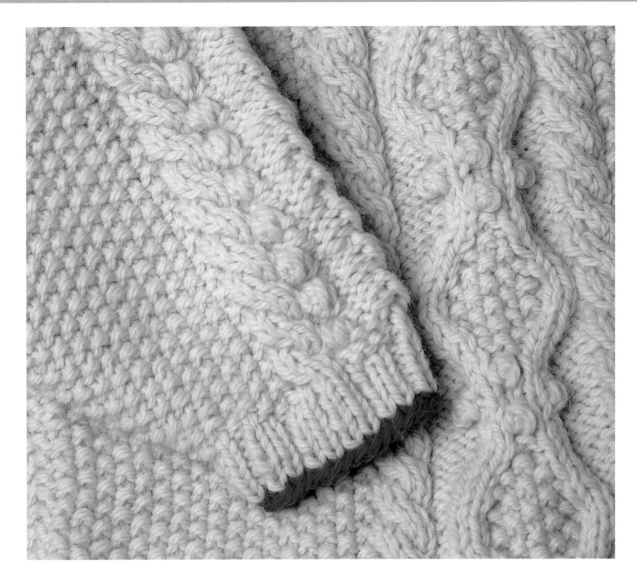

Next row (RS): Work seed st over first 17 (19, 23, 21, 23, 25, 29, 33, 35, 37) sts, work row 1 of cable panel A 1 (1, 1, 2, 2, 2, 2, 2, 2, 2) time, work row 1 of cable panel B, work row 1 of cable panel A 1 (1, 1, 2, 2, 2, 2, 2, 2, 2) time, and work seed st on rem 17 (19, 23, 21, 23, 25, 29, 33, 35, 37) sts. Cont working patts as set through row 20 of fourth (5 of fifth, 20 of fifth, 12 of sixth, 20 of sixth, 12 of seventh, 5 of eighth, 12 of eighth, 5 of ninth, 12 of ninth) vertical repeat of cable panel B—approx 13 (14, 16¼, 18¼, 19½, 21½, 23½, 24¾, 26¾, 28) in. Put first 15 (16, 20, 21, 23, 24, 28, 32, 32, 34) sts onto holder, then put center 29 (31, 31, 37, 37, 39, 39, 39, 43, 43) sts onto second holder, and then put rem 15 (16, 20, 21, 23, 24, 28, 32, 32, 34) sts onto third holder for later.

Front

Work as for back through row 8 of fourth (14 of fourth, 8 of fifth, 20 of fifth, 8 of sixth, 14 of sixth, 6 of seventh, 14 of seventh, 6 of eighth, 14 of eighth) vertical repeat of cable panel B—approx 11 (12, 14¼, 16¼, 17½, 18½, 20½, 21¾, 23¾, 25) in.

Shape neck: Patt 22 (24, 28, 30, 32, 35, 39, 43, 44, 46) sts, work 2 tog and turn. Cont on these sts only, and dec 1 st at neck edge every row, while maintaining patt, until 15 (16, 20, 21, 23, 24, 28, 32, 32, 34) sts rem. Work these sts, if necessary, until piece measures the same as the back, and put sts onto holder. Put center 11 (11, 11, 15, 15, 13, 13, 13, 15, 15) sts onto a holder for later. Join yarn to rem 24 (26, 30, 32, 34, 37, 41, 45, 46, 48) sts at neck edge, work 2 tog, patt to end. Cont as set, decreasing 1 st at neck edge every row, finishing as you did for first shoulder, and leaving sts on holder.

Sleeves

With size 8 needle and CC, CO 29 (32, 32, 35, 35, 38, 38, 41, 41, 41) sts, using same CO method used for front and back. Change to MC, p 1 row.

Next row (RS)—establish rib: K2, *p1, k2; rep from * to end.

Next row: P2, *k1, p2; rep from * to end. These 2 rows form rib. Work as set for 1¼ (1¼, 1¼, 1¼, 1¼, 1¼, 2, 2, 2, 2) in., ending with a RS row.

Next row (inc if indicated–this ensures that cable panel will center nicely above rib): Rib 14 (16, 16, 17, 17, 19, 19, 20, 20, 20), make 0 (1, 1, 0, 0, 1, 1, 0, 0, 0), and rib rem 15 (16, 16, 18, 19, 19, 21, 21, 21, 21) as established—29 (33, 33, 35, 35, 39, 39, 41, 41, 41) sts.

Next row (RS–establish cable patt): Change to size 10 needles, and work seed st over first 7 (9, 9, 10, 10, 12, 12, 13, 13, 13) sts, work row 1 cable panel A, p3, work row 1 cable panel A, and work seed st over rem 7 (9, 9, 10, 10, 12, 12, 13, 13, 13) sts.

Next row (WS): Seed st 7 (9, 9, 10, 10, 12, 12, 13, 13, 13) sts, work row 2 cable panel A, k3, work row 2 cable panel A, and seed st rem 7 (9, 9, 10, 10, 12, 12, 13, 13, 13) sts.

Next row (RS): Seed st 7 (9, 9, 10, 10, 12, 12, 13, 13, 13) sts, work row 3 cable panel A, p1, make bobble, p1, work row 3 cable panel A, and seed st to end.

Cont with patt as established, making bobble at center every fourth row (every cable twist row).

At the same time, shape sleeve, and inc 1 st each end third row, then every other row 5 (3, 3, 2, 1, 0, 0, 0, 0, 0) times, then every fourth row 6 (8, 10, 12, 14, 9, 8, 7, 8, 9) times, and then every sixth row 0 (0, 0, 0, 0, 5, 7, 8, 8, 8) times to 53 (57, 61, 65, 67, 69, 71, 73, 75, 77) sts. Work until sleeve measures 9 (10, 11, 12, 13, 14¼) in. for size 1 (3, 5, 7, 9, 12), 15½ (16, 16½, 17) for women's S (M, L, XL), and 17 (17½, 18, 18½) for men's S (M, L, XL). BO all sts.

Finishing

Weave in ends. Block or lightly steam pieces. Ktog shoulder seams as follows: With RSs facing each other, place the sts from the left front and back shoulder each onto a size 10 dpn, and hold the 2 needles parallel to each other. Insert a third dpn into the first st on the first needle as if to k, then into the first st on the second needle as if to k, and k the 2 sts as one. Rep this a second time—there should now be 2 sts on the right needle. *Pass the first st on the right needle over the second and BO.* K the next set of sts on the parallel dpns together, and rep from * to *. Cont in this way, knitting the corresponding sts of each shoulder tog and binding off as you go, until 1 st rem on right needle. Break yarn, and pull through last st to secure.

Neckband: With size 8 circ needle and MC and starting at back neck, k across 29 (31, 31, 37, 37, 39, 39, 39, 43, 43) sts from holder, pick up and k 13 (15, 15, 13, 13, 17, 17, 17, 16, 16) sts down left front neck, k across the 11 (11, 11, 15, 15, 13, 13, 13, 15, 15) sts from center front holder, and pick up and k 13 (15, 15, 13, 13, 15, 15, 15, 16, 16) sts up right front neck—66 (72, 72, 78, 78, 84, 84, 84, 90, 90) sts. Pm, join, and work rib: k2 (0, 0, 0, 0, 2, 2, 2, 2, 2), [p1, k2] around, ending rnd with p1 (0, 0, 0, 0, 1, 1, 1, 1, 1). Cont rib as set for 1¼ (1¼, 1¼, 1¼, 1¼, 1½, 1½, 1½, 1½, 1½) in. Break yarn, attach CC, and k 1 rnd. BO next rnd. Secure end, and weave in to give neckband a seamless finish. Center sleeves on shoulder seams with RSs facing, pin, and sew in place. Sew side and sleeve seams. Lightly steam seams.

BLANKET STATEMENT

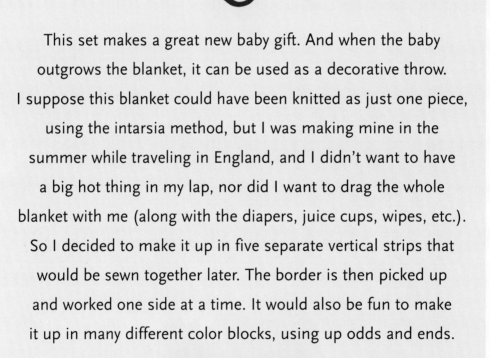

This set makes a great new baby gift. And when the baby
outgrows the blanket, it can be used as a decorative throw.
I suppose this blanket could have been knitted as just one piece,
using the intarsia method, but I was making mine in the
summer while traveling in England, and I didn't want to have
a big hot thing in my lap, nor did I want to drag the whole
blanket with me (along with the diapers, juice cups, wipes, etc.).
So I decided to make it up in five separate vertical strips that
would be sewn together later. The border is then picked up
and worked one side at a time. It would also be fun to make
it up in many different color blocks, using up odds and ends.

BLANKET STATEMENT

Checkered Baby Blanket with Matching Hat

∴ **MATERIALS**

Blanket

4 50g skeins Tahki Cotton Classic (108 yd./skein) in red #3407 (A), 3 skeins in white #3003 (B), and 1 skein in blue #3839 (C), or yarn that will knit to the gauge given below

Size 7 (4.5mm) needles, or size needed to match gauge given below

Size 5 (3.75mm) 24-in. circ needle for working border

Row counter, if desired

3½-in. cardboard rectangle for making tassels

Hat

1 skein C, small amount of A
Size 5 and 7 needles

Set

4 skeins A, 3 skeins B, and 2 skeins C

∴ SIZE

Newborn to 6 months
Blanket: 25 by 29½ in.
Hat circumference: 15 in.

∴ GAUGE

20 sts and 30 rows to 4 in./10cm over st st on size 7
needles
Don't waste precious time and precious yarn—make
a gauge swatch before beginning!

∴ PATTERN STITCH

Seed st

All rows: K1, *p1, K1; rep from * to end.

BLANKET

This baby blanket is made up of five vertical strips
that are knit separately and then sewn together.
Follow the chart for color-block patt, making three
7-block strips that beg and end with color A and
two 7-block strips that beg and end with color B.

Blanket strips

With size 7 needles and A, CO 25 sts. Work 30-row
patt from chart. Cut yarn, rejoin color B, and rep
30-row chart. Cont with st patt and color-block patt
as set for a total of 7 color blocks; BO. Work 2 more
strips identical to this one, and 2 strips that beg and
end with color B.

Finishing

When five strips have been completed, weave in
loose ends. Lightly steam to block, and flatten curled
edges. Carefully pin strips together as indicated in
diagram, lining up color breaks. Sew the four seams.
Lightly steam seams.

ST PATT CHART (25 sts)

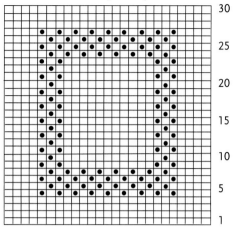

☐ K on RS, P on WS
⊡ P on RS, K on WS

Note: There are 4 rows of st st on
bottom of block, and 3 rows on top.
It may seem strange, but it looks
even this way.

Red	White	Red	White	Red
White	Red	White	Red	White
Red	White	Red	White	Red
White	Red	White	Red	White
Red	White	Red	White	Red
White	Red	White	Red	White
Red	White	Red	White	Red

29½"

25"

Border

Starting at the lower right corner of the blanket, work right vertical edging as follows: With RS facing, use size 5 circ needle to pick up and k 154 sts (22 sts/color block) up to top right corner. Work 6 rows seed st. BO in patt. Rep for left vertical edging, only beg at top left corner.

Bottom edge border: With RS facing, pick up and k 4 sts along lower edge of left vertical border, then 120 sts along lower edge of blanket (24 sts/per block), and then 4 more sts along lower edge of right vertical border (128 sts total). Work 6 rows seed st, and BO in patt.

Rep for top edge, beg top right. Weave in loose ends, and steam edges.

Tassels (make 4)

Wrap yarn A around the 3½-in. cardboard form about 50 times. Cut end. With yarn still wrapped around cardboard, take a 10-in. length of A, and pull it through the bottom edge bet the cardboard and the wrapped strands. Tie it tightly in a knot to secure bottom of tassel. Leave tail for sewing to blanket later. Now insert scissors into the top edge bet the cardboard and the wrapped strands, and cut to free the tassel. Cut a short length of yarn B, wrap it around strands a few times about 1 in. up from tail, and tie in a knot. Thread these ends up through center of tassel to conceal them, and snip strands shorter than tassel. Sew tassels to blanket corners using tail threaded into a tapestry needle. Bring ends up through center of tassel to conceal. Snip to same length as tassel ends.

HAT

Rolled-up brim: For newborn, use size 5 needles for brim, and for 3–6 months, use size 7 needles for brim. With A, CO 67 sts. Work st st for 12 rows. Change to C (and to size 7 needles if you started with the smaller needles), and k, increasing 8 sts evenly across to 75 sts.

Next row (WS): Beg with a p row, work three rows of st st.

Next row (RS): Work 3 repeats of row 5 of chart across row.
Cont working 3 repeats of st chart across as set, through row 30.

Shape crown (RS): *K1, k2tog; rep from * to end—50 sts. P 1 row.

Next row: *K2tog, k3; rep from * across to 40 sts.

Next row: *P2, p2tog; rep from * across to 30 sts.

Next row: *K2tog, k1; rep from * across to 20 sts.

Next row: P2tog across to 10 sts.

Next row: K2tog across to 5 sts. Cut yarn, leaving a long enough tail to sew back seam, pull through rem sts, and tighten. Sew back seam, reversing and using red for rolled brim. Weave in loose ends.

CANDY STRIPES

I designed the hat first for this set. I was thinking
of an oversized railroad engineer's cap, combined with
one of those funky hats from the '70s. Doing the hat inspired
the coveralls, which are knit on a circular needle around
the middle. The buttons at the chest are on the suspender
straps, so the length can be adjusted for varying heights.
My daughter Isabel modeled these in an orange, red,
and white combination when she was about 18 months old
and still in diapers. I designed them so that the insides
of the legs would button and unbutton for easy changing.
Try knitting them in wool for a warm winter outfit.

CANDY STRIPES

Unisex Striped Cotton Overalls with Matching Cap

Overalls (two color ways)

3 (4, 4, 4) 50g skeins Tahki Cotton Classic (108 yd./
skein) in blue #3873 or red #3997 (A)
2 (2, 2, 3) skeins lime green #3726 or orange
#3401 (B)
1 (1, 1, 1) skein red #3424 or natural white #3003 (C)
Size 3 (3.25mm) knitting needles
Size 6 (4mm) knitting needles, or size needed to
match gauge given below
Size 6 circ needle, 24 in.
Tapestry needle, stitch holders
Four ⅞-in. buttons for bodice and straps
Six ⅝-in. buttons for inside leg button band
(optional)

Cap (two color ways)

1 skein each A, B, and C
One 1-in. button for top

∵ SIZES

6 months (12–18 months; 2, 3 years)
Length: 19½ (21¾, 23½, 25½) in.
Chest: 21¾ (22½, 24, 24¾) in.
Hat circumference: S-16 (M-16¾, L-17¼) in.

∵ GAUGE

22 sts and 28 rows to 4 in. or 10cm in st st on size 6
needles
Don't waste precious time and precious yarn—make
a gauge swatch before beginning!

∵ PATTERN STITCHES

Stripe pattern

6 (7, 8, 9) rows B, 6 (7, 8, 9) rows A in st st

OVERALLS

Legs (make two)

With size 3 needles and A, CO 82 (85, 88, 91) sts.
Work in g st (k every row) for ¾ (1, 1, 1) in., ending
with WS row. Change to size 6 needles and B.
Beg with a k row, work stripe patt for 6 stripes
(above g st cuff), ending with a full A-colored stripe.

Shape crotch: Maintaining stripe patt, BO 3 sts
beg next two rows, and then dec 1 st beg next four
rows. Finish full B stripe.
Put rem 72 (75, 78, 81) sts onto holder for later.
Make second leg as first.

Body

Sl sts from both legs onto the circ needle to beg
working in the round—144 (150, 156, 162) sts. With
RS facing and A, join rnd, pm for center back, and
beg knitting every rnd, maintaining stripe patt, for
5 more stripes. (There should be 12 stripes total
above g st cuff.)

13th stripe (in color B): K2 (2, 2, 3) rnds even.

3rd (3rd, 3rd, 4th) rnd: *K22 (23, 24, 25), k2tog*;
rep from * to * 5 times.

4th (4th, 4th, 5th) rnd: *K21 (22, 23, 24), k2tog*;
rep from * to * 5 times.

5th (5th, 5th, 6th) rnd: *K20 (21, 22, 23), k2tog*;
rep from * to * 5 times.

6th (6th, 6th, 7th) rnd: *K19 (20, 21, 22), k2tog*;
rep from * to * 5 times—120 (126, 132, 138)
sts. Work even on next 0 (1, 2, 2) rnds to
complete stripe.
Change to A, and work 2 more rnds, decreasing
2 sts in second rnd for second and fourth sizes
only by [k40 (44), k2tog] twice, k to end. For first
and third sizes, simply k these 2 rnds even—
120 (124, 132, 136) sts.

Divide bodice

Put first 30 (31, 33, 34) and last 30 (31, 33, 34) sts onto
size 6 straight needle for bodice back. Put rem 60 (62,
66, 68) sts onto large holder for front bodice.

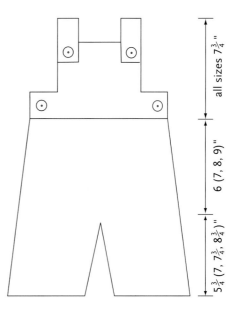

Back: Working back and forth in A only and beg
with a k row, work 14 rows. BO 8 sts beg next
2 rows. Cont on 44 (46, 50, 52) sts until back
measures 6 (6¼, 6¼, 6¼) in. from end of last B
stripe, ending with a WS row.

Divide for straps: K 10 sts for first strap, join second ball A, BO center 24 (26, 30, 32) sts, k rem
10 sts for second strap. Work both shoulder straps
simultaneously. P 1 row even.

Next row (RS): Dec 1 st at neck edges of each
strap (9 sts).
P one row even.

Next row: Dec 1 st each neck edge again to 8 sts.
P one row. Changing to size 3 needles and still
working both straps at the same time, beg working g st for 3¾ (3¾, 3¼, 3¼) in.

Make buttonholes: K3, yo, k2tog, k3. Work 1 in.
more in g st. BO straps.

Front: Put 60 (62, 66, 68) sts from holder onto
straight size 6 needles, and using A only, work
10 rows.

Make buttonholes: K4, k2tog, yo, work to last
6 sts, yo, k2tog, and k4. Work 3 more rows. BO
8 sts beg next 2 rows. Cont on 44 (46, 50, 52) sts

sts 7¼ (7¼, 7½, 7½) in. down from division of front and back bodice, centered on side of pant leg. With size 6 needles and C, work these sts in st st for 4 (4, 4¼, 4¼) in., ending with a RS row. Work 3 rows g st to prevent pocket top from curling; BO. Press pockets, pin sides in place, and sew onto pant legs.

Button bands on inside legs

Sew crotch seams. Weave in loose ends along inner leg edges.

Button band: With RSs facing and beg at bottom of cuff on back left leg, use size 3 needle and A to pick up and k 28 (35, 42, 49) sts up leg and another 28 (35, 42, 49) sts down to bottom of cuff on right back leg—56 (70, 84, 98) sts, or 4 (5, 6, 7) sts per stripe including cuff. Work 2 rows g st.

3rd row: K5 (5, 6, 7), p to last 5 (5, 6, 7) sts, and k them.

4th row: K all sts.

5th row: Rep row three.
K two rows; BO.

Buttonhole band: Work as for button band, picking up 56 (70, 84, 98) sts from bottom of cuff on right front around to bottom of cuff on left front. Work first 3 rows as for button band.

4th row: K9 (11, 14, 16), yo, k2tog, k6 (8, 10, 12), yo, k2tog, k6 (8, 10, 12), yo, k2tog, k3 (4, 4, 6), yo, k2tog, k6 (8, 10, 12), yo, k2tog, k6 (8, 10, 12), yo, k2tog, and k rem 8 (11, 14, 16) sts.

5th row: Rep row three.
K two rows; BO.

until front measures 3½ (3½, 4, 4) in. from end of last B stripe. Change to size 3 needles, and work in g st for 1 in. more. BO sts.

Pockets

Before picking up pocket sts, lay the overalls flat on an ironing board, cover with a light cloth, and lightly steam press entire garment.

Pockets (make 2): Using size 3 needle, weave needle under and over sts to pick up 30 (30, 32, 32)

If you don't care to have button bands along inside legs for easy diaper changes, simply sew inside leg seams at this point, and skip ahead to finishing.

5th row: K15 (16, 16), m1, *k29 (30, 31), m1*; rep from * to * twice, k14 (14, 15)—120 (124, 128) sts. Cont without further shaping to complete five full stripes (above g st band). Change to A—the remainder of the hat will be worked in A only. (For medium size only: P the next row at this point so that you can beg decreasing on a RS row.)

1st dec row: *K2, k2tog*; rep from * to * to end—90 (93, 96) sts.

2nd row: P.

3rd row: *K2, k2tog*; rep from * to * to end, k2 (1, 0)—68 (70, 72) sts.

4th row: P.

5th row: *K2, k2tog*; rep from * to * to end, k0 (2, 0)—51 (53, 54) sts.

6th row: P.

7th row: *K2, k2tog*; rep from * to * to end, k3 (1, 2)—39 (40, 41) sts.

8th row: P.

9th row: K2tog across, k1 (0, 1)—20 (20, 21) sts.

10th row: P.

11th row: K2tog across—10 (10, 11) sts. Cut yarn, leaving enough to pull through rem sts. Tighten, and knot in place.

Visor

Place markers 4 in. in from each end on garter band. Working from RS with size 6 needle and C, pick up and k 34 (36, 38) sts. Work in g st for 1 in. Continuing in g st, dec 1 st each end every other row 4 times to 26 (28, 30) sts. BO 3 sts beg next 2 rows to 20 (22, 24) sts. BO 5 sts beg next 2 rows to 10 (12, 14) sts. BO all sts.

Finishing

Weave in all ends. Sew back seam. Separate a short length of color B into 5 ply, and use for button thread, as you did for overalls. Sew button to center top. Using a tapestry needle and A, work blanket stitching along outer edge of visor.

Finishing

Weave in all loose ends. To sew buttons, cut a few 15-in. to 20-in. lengths of color B, and separate the 5 ply to use as thread. If you made the button band on inner legs, sew the 6 buttons opposite those buttonholes. Button these to hold legs in place, and sew tog g st cuff corners, keeping them overlapped as with button bands. Sew the 4 larger buttons opposite the buttonholes on the bodice.

HAT

Body

With size 3 needles and A, CO 88 (92, 96) sts. Work g st for 1 in., increasing to 108 (112, 116) sts evenly across last row, ending with a WS row. Change to larger needles and B, and beg stripe patt [6 (7, 8) rows/stripe], increasing as follows.

1st row: K13 (14, 14), m1, *k27 (28, 29), m1*; rep from * to * twice, k14 (14, 15).

2nd row: P.

3rd row: K14 (15, 15), m1, *k28 (29, 30), m1*; rep from * to * twice, k14 (14, 15).

4th row: P.

FALL COLORS

This unisex Fair Isle V-neck cardigan is knit as one piece for the body, with only the sleeves to sew on. There is a different color pattern on each section in one of my favorite color combinations. It looks more complex than it is—the color patterns are only 4 to 6 stitch repeats—so they're fairly mindless. And because the color work is done in the same two colors for the whole piece, there are not a million ends to weave in later. I couldn't find any buttons that I liked to go with the sweater when it was finished, so I made some out of Fimo modeling clay. It is very easy to work with, comes in a wide range of colors, and can be baked in a regular oven. The matching ribbed scarf is knit on large needles, so it goes very quickly.

FALL COLORS

Fair Isle V-Neck Cardigan with Matching Scarf

Cardigan

2 (3, 4, 5, 5, 6, 7) 50g balls Jo Sharp DK Wool
(107 yd./98m per ball) in Wattle #303 (A), 2 (3, 4,
4, 5, 6, 7) balls in Olive #313 (B), and 1 ball in Coral
#304 (C), or other DK yarn that will knit to the
gauge given below
5 (5, 5, 5, 5, 7, 7) ½-in. buttons
Size 6 (4mm) straight and circ knitting needles
(24 in. to 29 in.), or size needed to match gauge
given below
Size 3 (3mm) straight and circ needles (24 in. to 29 in.)
for working ribbing and picking up button bands
Three size 6 dpns for working shoulder seams
Tapestry needle, stitch holders, row counter

Scarf

1 ball each C and A and leftover B for pom-poms
Size 9 (5.5mm) knitting needles
1-in. commercial pom-pom maker (Clover makes
a good one)

Set

3 (3, 4, 5, 6, 7, 8) balls A, 2 (3, 4, 5, 5, 6, 7) balls B,
and 2 balls C

⋮ SIZES

6 months (1–2, 3–4, 5–6, 7–8, 9–10, 11–12 years)
Length: 10½ (12½, 14½, 15½, 16½, 18, 19) in.
Chest: 22½ (26, 29, 33, 36, 39, 43) in.
Sleeve: 7½ (9½, 11, 12½, 14, 15½, 17) in.
Scarf length: S-32 (M-34, L-37) in.

⋮ GAUGE

27 sts and 26 rows to 4 in./10cm over color patts on
size 6 (4mm) needles
Generic gauge—5½ sts/in. in st st on size 6 needles
Don't waste precious time and precious yarn—make
a gauge swatch before beginning!

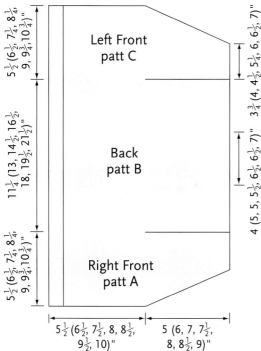

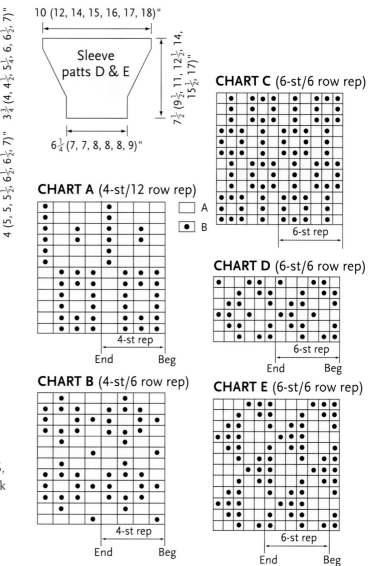

CHART A (4-st/12 row rep)

□ A

● B

4-st rep

End   Beg

CHART B (4-st/6 row rep)

4-st rep

End   Beg

CHART C (6-st/6 row rep)

6-st rep

CHART D (6-st/6 row rep)

6-st rep

End   Beg

CHART E (6-st/6 row rep)

6-st rep

End   Beg

CARDIGAN

Body

With size 3 circ needle and C, CO 152 (176, 196, 220, 244, 264, 288) sts. Work in k2, p2 rib back and forth for 3 rows.

Next row (WS): Change to A, and p across.

Next row (RS): K2, p2 across in A.

Next row (WS): Change back to C, and p all sts. In C, work in k2, p2 rib a further 2 rows, ending with a WS row and increasing 1 st at center of last row to 153 (177, 197, 221, 245, 265, 289) sts. Change to larger size 6 needle and A and B. Work row 1 of patt from chart A across first 36 (42, 54, 60, 66, 72) sts for right front, k2 sts in B for division bet right front and back, work row 1 of patt from chart B across center 77 (89, 97, 109, 121, 129, 141) sts for back, k2 in B for division bet back and left front, and then work row 1 of patt from chart C across rem 36 (42, 48, 54, 60, 66, 72) sts for left front.

Next row (WS): P row 2 of patt from chart C across first 36 (42, 48, 54, 60, 66, 72) sts for left front, p2 in B for division bet left front and back, p row 2 of patt from chart B across center 77 (89, 97, 109, 121, 129, 141) sts for back, p2 in B for division bet back and right front, and p row 2 of patt from chart A across rem 36 (42, 48, 54, 60, 66, 72) sts for right front. Cont working body with patts as set until piece measures 5½ (6½, 7½, 8, 8½, 9½, 10) in. from beg, ending with a WS row.

Upper right front

Separate for armholes, and shape right front V-neck simultaneously—next row (RS): Ssk, patt across next 34 (40, 46, 52, 58, 64, 70) sts, k1 in B (first of the 2 division sts). Put rem 116 (134, 148, 166, 184, 198, 216) sts onto holders. Cont on right front sts only, and maintain patt, decreasing 1 st by ssk beg every RS row 8 (12, 14, 15, 17, 20, 22) more times, and then beg every sixth row 2 times to 26 (28, 32, 37, 41, 44, 48) sts (including the division st). Work in patt without further shaping until front measures 10½ (12½, 14½, 15½, 16½, 18, 19) in. from beg, ending with a WS row. (Make note of row number.) Put these right front shoulder sts onto holder for later finishing.

Upper left front

Sl sts from holder for left front (patt C) plus 1 st from the 2 dividing sts onto size 6 needles—37 (43, 49, 55, 61, 67, 73) sts total. Beg with a RS row, k1 B (division st), patt 34 (40, 46, 52, 58, 64, 70), k2tog. Cont on patt as set, decreasing 1 st at neck edge ending every RS row 8 (12, 14, 15, 17, 20, 22) more times, and then ending every sixth row 2 times to 26 (28, 32, 37, 41, 44, 48) sts (including the division st). Work in patt without further shaping until left front measures same as right front and ends with the same row number. Put shoulder sts onto holder.

Upper back

Put the back sts from the holder plus the dividing st on each end onto needle—79 (91, 99, 111, 123, 131, 143) sts total. Beg with a RS row, k1 in B (division st), patt 77 (89, 97, 109, 121, 129, 141), and k1 in B (division st).

Cont working patt as set without shaping until back measures same as fronts and ends with same row number. Put first 26 (28, 32, 37, 41, 44, 48) sts from back onto size 6 dpn, put center 27 (35, 35, 37, 41, 43, 47) sts for neck onto a holder for later, and put rem 26 (28, 32, 37, 41, 44, 48) sts from back onto a second holder. Put right front shoulder sts onto second size 6 dpn. With a third dpn, ktog shoulder seam as follows: Hold the 2 needles with stitches on them parallel, with RSs facing each other. Insert a third dpn into the first st on the first needle as if to k, then into the first st on the second needle as if to k, and, using yarn A, k the 2 sts as one. Rep this a second time—there should now be 2 sts on the right needle. *Pass the first st on the right needle over the second, and BO.* K the next set of sts on the dpns tog, and rep from * to *. Cont in this way, knitting the corresponding sts of each shoulder tog and binding off as you go, until 1 st rem on the right needle. Break yarn, and pull through last st to secure. Rep this process for left shoulder.

Sleeves

With size 3 needles and C, CO 42 (48, 48, 54, 54, 54, 60) sts. Work rib as for body. Change to size 6 needles, and work color patt from chart D for 6 rows.

Next row—inc (RS): K1 in A, m1 in B by picking up the horizontal strand bet the last and next st; beg patt from chart E where indicated on chart, patt across until 1 st rem, m1 in A, k last st in B. This will ensure that patts D and E line up properly. Cont with patt as set, increasing 1 st each end every RS row 9 (11, 20, 15, 16, 20, 15) more times, and then every fourth row 3 (5, 3, 8, 10, 10, 15) times to 68 (82, 96, 102, 108, 116, 122) sts. Cont on sleeve without further shaping until it measures 7½ (9½, 11, 12½, 14, 15½, 17) in. from beg; BO.

Buttonhole/button bands

With size 3 needle and C, starting at lower right front edge on RS, pick up and k31 (37, 43, 46, 49, 54, 57) sts up to beg of neck shaping, pick up and k31 (37, 43, 45, 48, 52, 55) sts from beg neck shaping to shoulder seam, k across first 13 (17, 17, 18, 20, 21, 23) sts from holder for neck, k next 2 sts from holder tog, k across rem 12 (16, 16, 17, 19, 20, 22) sts from holder, pick up and k31 (37, 43, 45, 48, 52, 55) sts down neck shaping, and pick up and k31 (37, 43, 46, 49, 54, 57) sts down left front to bottom—150 (182, 206, 218, 234, 254, 270) sts total. Work rib as follows:

Row 1 and all odd-numbered rows (WS): P2, *k2, p2; rep from * to end.

Row 2 (RS): K2, *p2, k2; rep from * to end.

Row 4 (buttonhole row): Change to yarn A, and k all sts, working buttonholes as follows: If cardigan is for a girl—k3, *yo, k2tog, k5 (6, 7, 8, 9, 6, 7)*; rep from * to * 3 (3, 3, 3, 3, 5, 5) more times, yo, k2tog, and k to end of row. If for a boy—k117 (145, 165, 173, 185, 201, 211), *k2tog, yo, k5 (6, 7, 8, 9, 6, 7)*; rep from * to * 3 (3, 3, 3, 3, 5, 5) times, k2tog, yo, and k3.

Row 5: As for row one, only still in yarn A.

Row 6 (RS): Change back to yarn C, and k across.

Row 8: As for row 2.

Row 9: BO in rib patt.

Finishing

Weave in loose ends. Lightly steam body and sleeve pieces to block, avoiding ribbing. Center sleeve tops on shoulder seams with RSs facing each other, and pin sleeves evenly around armhole. Backstitch sleeves to body. Sew inside sleeve seams. Lightly steam all seams. Sew buttons opposite buttonholes.

SCARF

With size 9 needle and C, CO 26 sts.

Row 1: K2, *p2, k2; rep from * to end.

Row 2: P2, *k2, p2; rep from * to end.
Rep rows one and two one more time.

Row 5: Change to yarn A, and rep row one. (Don't cut yarn C. You can carry the yarns up the side of the scarf by twisting the strands every other row.)

Row 6: Rep row 2, only still in yarn A. Cont working this 6-row stripe repeat for approx 32 (34, 37) in., ending with a full stripe in C. BO sts. Weave in loose ends. Make four 1-in. pom-poms in yarn B, leaving 10-in. tails to sew pom-poms to corners of scarf. After attaching, secure, pull tail up through center of pom-pom, and cut to hide end in pom-pom.

BOXED SET

This is a versatile cardigan and hat set that can
be knit in any color combination and in any fiber. I used
a heavy worsted-weight wool, which makes for a dense fabric
that holds its shape. The checkerboard pattern on the trim
is done in garter stitch, so you have to strand the yarns along
the front of the work when you are working the wrong side.
This technique feels a little funny at first, but once you get
the hang of it, it's a snap. The main part of the sweater
is worked in reverse stockinette stitch. One knitter told me
she made the reverse stockinette pieces on her knitting machine,
then picked up the stitches for the trim, and
worked those parts by hand. Not a bad idea if you get
bored by large areas of solid stockinette stitch.

BOXED SET

Unisex Cardigan and Hat with Checkered Garter Stitch Borders

⁖ MATERIALS

Cardigan

2 (2, 3, 3, 4, 5, 5, 6, 6, 7) 4-oz. skeins Peace Fleece Worsted (30% mohair, 70% wool, 200 yd./skein) in violet (A) and 1 (1, 1, 1, 1, 1, 1, 1, 1, 2) skein in red (B), or other worsted-weight yarn that will knit to gauge given below

Size 8 (5mm) knitting needles, or size needed to match gauge given below

Three size 8 dpns

Four stitch holders, row counter, tapestry needle

5 (5, 5, 5, 5, 7, 7, 7, 7, 9) 1-in. buttons to match A

Hat

1 skein each A and B

2-in. commercial pom-pom maker

Set

2 (3, 3, 4, 4, 5, 6, 7, 7, 8) skeins A and 1 (1, 1, 1, 2, 2, 2, 2, 2, 2) skein B

⁖ SIZES

6 months (1–2, 3–4, 5–6, 7–8, 9–10, 11–12 years; women's S, M, L)

Chest: 23 (27, 30, 32, 34, 37½, 41, 44½, 46, 50) in.

Length: 10½ (12½, 14, 15½, 16½, 17½, 18½, 21, 22½, 24) in.

Sleeve: 6½ (8½, 10, 11½, 13, 14½, 15, 15½, 16, 16½) in.

Hat circumference: S-18¼ (M-20, L-22½) in.

⁖ GAUGE

Generic yarn gauge: 16 sts and 24 rows/4 in. over RSS on size 8 (5mm) needles

Garter-stitch, check-pattern gauge: 18 sts and 28 rows/4 in. on size 8 needles

Don't waste precious time and precious yarn—make a gauge swatch before beginning!

⁖ PATTERN STITCH

The color patt is worked in g st (k on RS, k on WS). When working the RS rows, strand yarn at back of work as usual. When working WS rows, however, you will need to strand yarn at front of work.

CARDIGAN

Back

With size 8 needles and B, CO 54 (62, 70, 74, 78, 86, 94, 102, 106, 114) sts.

Row 1 (RS): K1B (selvage st), rep row 1 from chart across until 1 st rem, k1A (selvage st).

Row 2: K1A (selvage st), rep row two of chart across until 1 st rem, k1B (selvage st).
Cont working patt as established, with 1 selvage st worked in same color as adjacent check at each end of every row, through last row of chart.

Next row (RS): In A only, k 1 row, decreasing 8 (9, 10, 10, 10, 11, 12, 13, 14, 14) sts evenly across row to 46 (53, 60, 64, 68, 75, 82, 89, 92, 100) sts.

Next (WS): Beg with a k row, work back in RSS (k on WS, p on RS), until back measures 10½ (12½, 14, 15½, 16½, 17½, 18½, 21, 22½, 24) in. from beg, ending with a WS row.
Work across first 15 (18, 21, 22, 23, 25, 28, 31, 32, 35) sts, and put on holder, BO center 16 (17, 18, 20, 22, 25, 26, 27, 28, 30) sts for neck, work across rem 15 (18, 21, 22, 23, 25, 28, 31, 32, 35) sts, and put on holder for later.

Left front

With size 8 needles and B, CO 24 (28, 32, 34, 36, 40, 44, 48, 50, 54) sts.

Row 1 (RS): K1B (selvage), work row 1 of chart patt across until selvage st rem, k1B (k1B, k1B, k1A, k1B, k1B, k1B, k1B, k1A, k1A).

Row 2: K3B (k3B, k3B, k1A, k3B, k3B, k3B, k3B, k1A, k1A), work row two of chart patt across until 1 st rem, k1B (selvage).
Cont working patt as set, with 1 selvage st worked in same color as adjacent check at each end of every row, through last row of chart.

Next row (RS): In A only, k 1 row, decreasing 4 (4, 5, 5, 5, 6, 6, 6, 7, 7) sts evenly across row to 20 (24, 27, 29, 31, 34, 38, 42, 43, 47) sts.

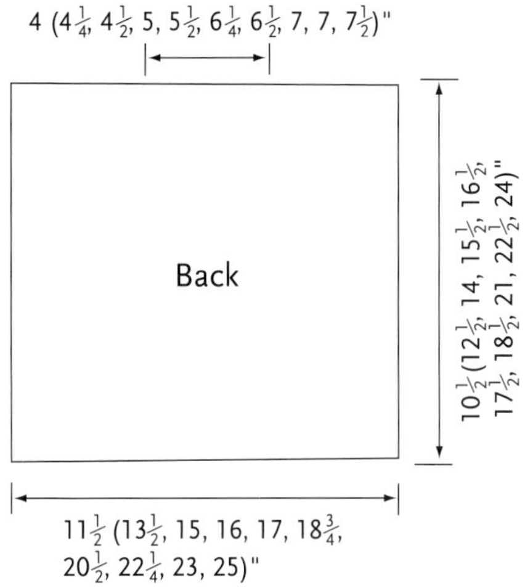

4 (4¼, 4½, 5, 5½, 6¼, 6½, 7, 7, 7½)"
Back
10½ (12½, 14, 15½, 16½, 17½, 18½, 21, 22½, 24)"
11½ (13½, 15, 16, 17, 18¾, 20½, 22¼, 23, 25)"

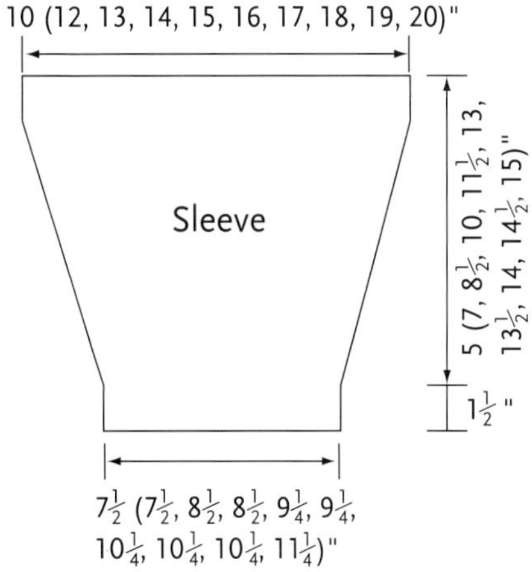

10 (12, 13, 14, 15, 16, 17, 18, 19, 20)"
Sleeve
5 (7, 8½, 10, 11½, 13, 13½, 14, 14½, 15)"
1½"
7½ (7½, 8½, 8½, 9¼, 9¼, 10¼, 10¼, 10¼, 11¼)"

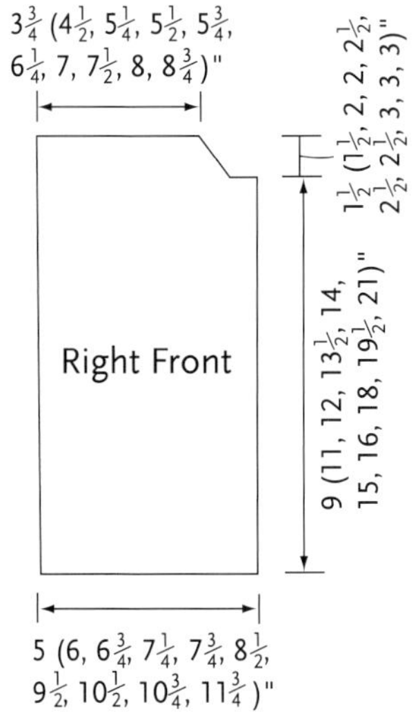

3¾ (4½, 5¼, 5½, 5¾, 6¼, 7, 7½, 8, 8¾)"
1½ (1½, 2, 2, 2½, 2½, 2½, 3, 3, 3)"
Right Front
9 (11, 12, 13½, 14, 15, 16, 18, 19½, 21)"
5 (6, 6¾, 7¼, 7¾, 8½, 9½, 10½, 10¾, 11¾)"

COLOR PATT
(4-st rep)

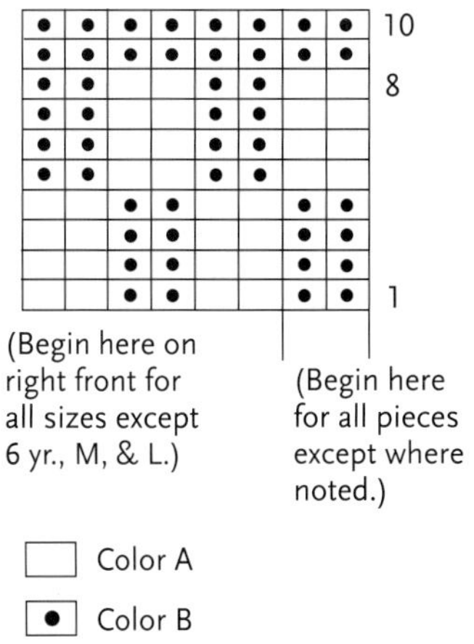

10
8
1
(Begin here on right front for all sizes except 6 yr., M, & L.)
(Begin here for all pieces except where noted.)
Color A
Color B

Next row (WS): Beg with k row, work remainder in RSS until front measures 9 (11, 12, 13½, 14, 15, 16, 18, 19½, 21) in. from beg, ending with RS row.

Shape neck (WS): BO 3 (4, 4, 4, 4, 5, 5, 5, 5, 6) sts beg this row, and then dec 1 st at neck edge beg every WS row 2 (2, 2, 3, 4, 4, 5, 6, 6, 6) times to 15 (18, 21, 22, 23, 25, 28, 31, 32, 35) sts. Work until piece measures same as back. Leave sts on holder, leaving a long tail to k shoulder seam.

Right front

Work as for left front, only beg first row of color patt with k2A, as indicated on chart for all sizes except 6-year, M, and L sizes, working selvage sts in same color as adjacent checks, and reversing neck shaping to beg of RS rows. Leave sts on holder, leaving a long tail to ktog shoulder seam.

Sleeves

With size 8 needle and B, CO 34 (34, 38, 38, 42, 42, 46, 46, 46, 50) sts. Work patt as for back through last row of chart.

> **Next row (RS):** K row in A, decreasing 4 sts evenly to 30 (30, 34, 34, 38, 38, 42, 42, 42, 46) sts. K next WS row.

Next row (RS): Beg with a p row, work sleeve in RSS, and inc 1 st each end this row, then every fourth row 1 (8, 4, 6, 3, 4, 3, 7, 11, 11) time, and then every sixth row 3 (0, 4, 4, 7, 8, 9, 7, 5, 5) times to 40 (48, 52, 56, 60, 64, 68, 72, 76, 80) sts.

Work without further shaping until sleeve measures 6½ (8½, 10, 11½, 13, 14½, 15, 15½, 16, 16½) in. from beg. BO, leaving a long tail to sew sleeve to body later.

Finishing

Use the bind-off seam technique for shoulder seams as follows: With RSs facing each other, place the sts from the left front and back shoulder each onto a size 8 dpn, and hold the needles parallel. Insert a third dpn into the first st on the first needle as if to k, then into the first st on the second needle as if to k, and k the 2 sts as one. Rep this a second time—there should now be 2 sts on the right needle. *Pass the first st on the right needle over the second, and BO*. K the next 2 sts on the parallel dpn tog, and rep from * to *. Cont in this way, knitting the corresponding sts of each shoulder tog and binding off as you go, until 1 st rem on the right needle. Break yarn, and pull through last st to secure. Rep this process for right shoulder.

Weave in loose ends, except for those that will be used to sew seams. Lightly steam press pieces to block, including shoulder seams.

> **Attach sleeves:** Center sleeve on armhole, and backstitch sleeve top to armhole edge with RSs facing each other.
>
> **Collar:** With size 8 needle and B and starting at left front neck edge with WS facing, pick up and k 13 (15, 16, 17, 18, 19, 20, 22, 22, 24) sts up to shoulder seam, 22 (22, 24, 26, 28, 32, 33, 36, 36, 38) sts across back, and 13 (15, 16, 17, 18, 19, 20, 22, 22, 24) sts down right front neck edge—48 (52, 56, 60, 64, 70, 74, 80, 80, 86) sts. K 1 row.
>
> **Next row (RS):** Work row one of chart, end k0 (0, 0, 0, 2, 2, 0, 0, 2) in color B.
>
> **Next row (WS):** K 0 (0, 0, 0, 0, 2, 2, 0, 0, 2) in color B, and work row two of chart.

Cont working patt as set through row eight. Rep rows one to eight 1 (1, 1, 2, 2, 2, 2, 3, 3, 3) more time, and then work rows one to four 1 (1, 1, 0, 0, 1, 1, 0, 0, 0) more time. Work last two rows of chart, binding off on last row.
Sew sleeve and side seams, and lightly steam.

Button band: With size 8 needle and B and starting at left front neck edge with RS facing, pick up and k 40 (50, 54, 60, 64, 68, 72, 82, 88, 94) sts down to hem. K 1 row.

Next row (RS): Rep row one of chart across, and end k0 (2, 2, 0, 0, 0, 0, 2, 0, 2) in B.

Next row (WS): K 0 (2, 2, 0, 0, 0, 0, 2, 0, 2) in B; then rep row 2 of chart across to end.
Cont working patt as set, through last row of chart, binding off on row 10.

Buttonhole band: Work as for button band, only beg at lower edge, and work through row four of patt chart.

Next row (buttonhole row): Maintaining patt, k3 (4, 4, 3, 3, 3, 3, 4, 4, 4), *BO 2, k6 (8, 9, 11, 12, 13, 14, 10, 11, 12)*; rep from * to * 3 (3, 3, 3, 3, 3, 3, 5, 5, 5) times, end BO 2, k3 (4, 4, 3, 3, 3, 3, 4, 4, 4). Finish from here as for button band, only CO 2 sts in patt over bound off sts on next row. Weave in all rem ends. Sew buttons opposite buttonholes using yarn or thread to match color B.

HAT
With size 8 needle and B, CO 82 (90, 102) sts.

Next row (RS): K1 B (selvage), rep row one of chart across row to last st, and end k1 A (selvage).

Next row (WS): K1 A, rep row two of chart across row, stranding yarns on WS, to last st, and k1 B.
Cont working patt as established with 1 selvage st each end worked in the same color as the adjacent patt st, through row eight. Rep rows one to eight 2 (2, 2½) more times.
In B only, k 2 rows, decreasing 1 st each end for first size to 80 sts, and 1 st each end for third size to 100 sts in second row.

Next row (RS): Change to A only, and *k2tog, k6 (7, 8)*; rep from * to * across—70 (80, 90) sts.

Next row: K even.

Next (RS) beg with a p row, work RSS from here, while shaping crown as follows.

Row 1: *P2tog, p5 (6, 7)*; rep from * to * across—60 (70, 80) sts.

Row 2 and all WS rows unless indicated: K even.

Row 3: *P2tog, p4 (5, 6)*; rep from * to * across—50 (60, 70) sts.

Cont shaping crown as established, decreasing 10 sts every RS row, evenly spaced, until 20 sts rem, ending with a WS row.

Next row (RS): P2tog across row—10 sts.

Next row (WS): K2tog across—5 sts.
Cut yarn, leaving a long enough tail to sew seam, pull yarn through rem 5 sts, tighten, and secure.

Finishing
Sew crown and back seams. Weave in loose ends. Make one 2-in. pom-pom, wrapping one-half of pom-pom maker in A and the other half in B. Sew pom-pom to center top of hat.

CHECKERED PAST

This set has proven to be one of the most popular and practical Monkeysuits. The sweater is the type of unfussy basic cardigan that can be worn every day. The sweater has very long sleeves and a full, cropped, boxy body so that it will fit a child for a few years. I made the smaller size for a friend's baby, and he wore it from birth to 2 years. (And he was a big boy.) Now my daughter Matilda is wearing it. The stitch pattern is the same on the wrong side as it is on the right side, so when you roll up the sleeves, the pockets don't look inside out. The set-in pockets are real, but for knitters who can't be bothered, the pockets can be eliminated. Just make sure you choose some nice juicy buttons that will highlight the accent color.

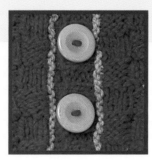

CHECKERED PAST

Unisex Check-Stitch Wool Cardigan with Matching Hat

∴ MATERIALS

Cardigan

4 (5, 5) 2-oz. skeins Alice Starmore Scottish Heather (Shetland wool, 120 yd./skein) in Lacquer #1220 (A) and 1 (1, 1) skein in Scotch Broom #116 (B), or yarn that will knit to the gauge given on facing page
Five 1-in. buttons to match B
Size 6 (4mm) knitting needles
Size 8 (5mm) knitting needles, or size needed to match gauge given on facing page
1 set size 8 dpns for shoulder seams

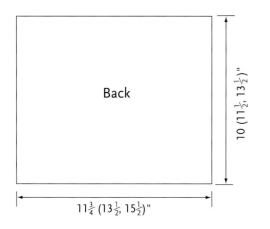

Back

$10 (11\frac{1}{2}, 13\frac{1}{2})$"

$11\frac{3}{4} (13\frac{1}{2}, 15\frac{1}{2})$"

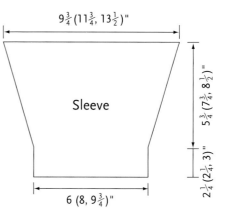

$3\frac{1}{2} (4\frac{1}{4}, 5)$"

$1\frac{3}{4}$"

Front

$8\frac{1}{4} (9\frac{3}{4}, 11\frac{3}{4})$"

$5\frac{3}{4} (6\frac{3}{4}, 7\frac{3}{4})$"

Size 6 circ needle for picking up collar stitches
Row counter, tapestry needle, and stitch holders

Hat

1 skein each A and B
Crochet hook and 3-in. cardboard rectangle for
making tassel

Set

5 (5, 6) skeins A, 1 skein B

∴ SIZES

3–9 months (1–2, 3–4 years)
Length: 10 (11½, 13½) in.
Chest: 23½ (27, 31) in.
Sleeve: 8 (10, 11½) in. (full length): 7 (9, 10) in. (with
cuff turned up)
Hat circumference: S-15½ (M-17½, L-19¼) in.

∴ GAUGE

17 sts and 28 rows to 4 in./10cm over check patt on
size 8 needles
Don't waste precious time and precious yarn—make
a gauge swatch before beginning!

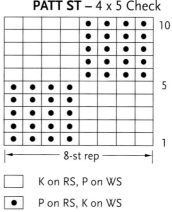

$9\frac{3}{4} (11\frac{3}{4}, 13\frac{1}{2})$"

Sleeve

$5\frac{3}{4} (7\frac{3}{4}, 8\frac{1}{2})$"

$2\frac{1}{4} (2\frac{1}{4}, 3)$"

$6 (8, 9\frac{3}{4})$"

PATT ST – 4 x 5 Check

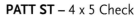

8-st rep

☐ K on RS, P on WS

⬛• P on RS, K on WS

CARDIGAN

Back
Using size 8 needles and A, CO 50 (58, 66) sts.

Rows 1 to 5: K1 (selvage st), work rows one to five of chart 6 (7, 8) times, end k1 (selvage st).

Rows 6 to 10: K1 (selvage st), work rows 6 to 10 of chart 6 (7, 8) times, end k1 (selvage st). Cont to work back with check patt as set with selvage st each end worked in g st until you reach row 69 (79, 94), approx 10 (11½, 13½) in.

Last row: Patt 15 (18, 21) sts and put on holder for later. BO 20 (22, 24) sts for neck purlwise, patt rem 15 (18, 21) sts, and put on holder, leaving a 25-in. tail for working shoulder seam.

Pocket linings

Right front lining
With size 8 needles and B, CO 12 (16, 16) sts. For S size, work right pocket lining as follows.

Rows 1 to 5: K2, p4, k4, p2.

Rows 6 to 10: P2, k4, p4, k2. Rep rows 1 to 5 to complete right lining. Leave sts on holder. For M size, work right pocket lining as follows.

Rows 1, 3, 5, 6, 8, and 10: P2, k4, p4, k4, p2.

Rows 2, 4, 7, and 9: K2, p4, k4, p4, k2. Rep rows 1 to 10 to complete right lining and leave sts on holder. For L size, work right pocket lining as follows:

Rows 1 to 5: *P4, k4; rep from * to end.

Rows 6 to 10: *K4, p4; rep from * to end.

Rep rows 1 to 10 to complete lining, and put sts on holder.

Left front pocket lining

CO same number of sts as for right lining. Work S and L left linings as you did for the right linings. Work M left lining as follows:

Rows 1, 3, 5, 6, 8, and 10: K2, p4, k4, p4, k2.

Rows 2, 4, 7, and 9: P2, k4, p4, k4, p2. Put sts on holder.

Right front

With size 8 needles and A, CO 25 (29, 33) sts.

Row 1: P0 (4, 0), work row one of chart 3 (3, 4) times, and end k1 (selvage st).

Row 2: K1 (selvage st), work second row of chart 3 (3, 4) times, and end k0 (4, 0). Cont to work check patt as set, with 1 selvage st worked in g st at end of RS rows and beg WS rows until you have completed 19 (24, 24) rows.

Work pocket openings WS (RS, RS): Work first 7 (6, 8) sts of patt (include selvage for smallest size), BO next 12 (16, 16) sts, and work rem 6 (7, 9) sts (include selvage for M and L).

Next row: Patt 6 (7, 9), k (p, p) across 12 (16, 16) sts of pocket lining from holder (to ensure clean color break), and patt rem 7 (6, 8) sts.
Work next row entirely in patt.
Cont working right front until you complete row 58 (68, 82)—8¼ (9¾, 11¾) in.

Shape neck: BO 6 (7, 8) sts beg next row and then 1 st beg every RS row 4 times. Work until front measures the same as the back. Put rem 15 (18, 21) sts onto holder to be worked later.

Left front

CO same number of sts as for right front.

Row 1: K1 (selvage), work row one of chart 3 (3, 4) times, and end k0 (4, 0).

Row 2: P0 (4, 0), work row two of chart 3 (3, 4) times, and end k1 (selvage). Cont to work check patt as set, with 1 selvage st worked in g st at beg

RS rows and end of WS rows until you have completed 19 (24, 24) rows.

Work pocket openings WS (RS, RS): Work first 6 (7, 9) sts of patt (include selvage for M and L), BO next 12 (16, 16) sts, and work rem 7 (6, 8) sts.

Next row: Work first 7 (6, 8) sts, k (p, p) across 12 (16, 16) sts of left front pocket lining from holder, and patt rem 6 (7, 9) sts.
Work remainder of left front as for right front, with 1 selvage st on opposite side, but reverse neck shaping to WS, beg neck shaping on row 58 (68, 82). Put rem 15 (18, 21) sts onto holder leaving a 20-in. tail for working shoulder seam later.

Sleeves

With size 8 needles and A, CO 26 (34, 42) sts.

Work cuff—rows 1 to 5: K1 (selvage), work rows 1 to 5 of chart 3 (4, 5) times, and end k1 (selvage).

Rows 6 to 10: K1 (selvage), work rows 6 to 10 of chart 3 (4, 5) times, and end k1 (selvage). Rep rows 1 to 5 (1 to 5, 1 to 10) once more to complete cuff, approx 2 (2, 3) in.

Shape sleeve: Inc 1 st each end next row, maintaining patt, then every fourth row 7 (4, 1) times, and then every eighth row 0 (3, 6) times to 42 (50, 58) sts. Cont working sleeve until you reach row 55 (70, 80)—approx 8 (10, 11½) in. from beg. BO in patt.

Button band

With RS facing and starting on the lower edge of right front, use size 6 needle and B to pick up and k 38 (46, 54) sts up to neck edge. K 1 row. Change to A, and k 1 row.

Next row: Work rib—p2, *k2, p2; rep from * to end.

Next row: K2, *p2, k2; rep from * to end. Rep these last two rows once more. BO in rib.

Buttonhole band

With RS facing and starting at neck edge of left front, use size 6 needle and B to pick up and k 38 (46, 54) sts down to lower edge. Work as for button band through first rib row.

Second rib row: Rib 2 (4, 4), BO 2, *rib 6 (7, 9), BO 2*; rep from * to * three more times, rib 2 (4, 4).

Third rib row: Rib 2 (4, 4), CO 2, *rib 6 (7, 9), CO 2*; rep from * to * three more times, rib 2 (4, 4). Work fourth rib row even, and then BO in rib.

Nehru collar

Before working collar, the shoulders need to be joined. Use the BO seam technique for shoulder seams as follows: With RSs facing each other, place the sts from the left front and back shoulder each onto a size 8 dpn, and hold the two needles parallel to each other. Insert a third dpn into the first st on the first needle as if to k, then into the first st on the second needle as if to k, and k the 2 sts as one. Rep this a second time—there should now be 2 sts on the right needle. *Pass the first st on the right needle over the second, and BO.* K the next set of sts on the parallel dpns tog, and rep from * to *. Cont in this way, knitting the corresponding sts of each shoulder tog and binding off as you go, until 1 st remains on the right needle. Break yarn, and pull through last st to secure. Rep this process for right shoulder.

Collar: Take size 6 circ needle and B, with RS facing, and beg where you picked up the sts for the button band with yarn B, pick up and k 17 (18, 19) sts from right neck edge up to shoulder seam, 24 (26, 28) sts across back, 17 (18, 19) sts down left front to neck edge, stopping where you picked up the sts for the buttonhole band with yarn B— 58 (62, 66) sts.

Row 1 (WS): P2, *k2, p2; rep from * to end.

Row 2: K2, *p2, k2; rep from * to end. Rep these last two rows two more times, binding off in patt on last row.

Finishing

Weave in loose ends. Pin and backstitch sleeves in place. Lay sweater flat, and steam—do not press. Sew inside sleeve seams, reversing for cuff if

desired. Sew side seams. Pin pocket linings to WS fronts, matching up patt, and stitch in place. Using a tapestry needle and B, work chain st across right and left front pocket tops (see p. 25). Sew five buttons to button band opposite buttonholes. Very lightly steam seams.

HAT

With size 6 needle and B, CO 66 (74, 82) sts. Attach row counter to your needle. Work in st st for 2 in., ending with a RS row. Change to A and size 8 needles, and p 1 row.

Row 1: K1 (selvage), work first row of chart for 8 (9, 10) repeats, and end k1 (selvage).

Row 2: K1 (selvage), work second row of chart for 8 (9, 10) repeats, and end k1 (selvage). Cont working check patt as established, with 1 selvage st on each end, until you reach row 25, approx 3½ in. to 3¾ in., from beg A. Shape crown as follows, maintaining chart patt around decreases. The selvage sts are included in the st counts.

Row 26: K1 (selvage), patt 6, work 2 tog in patt twice, patt 12 (12, 16), work 2 tog in patt twice, patt 12 (20, 20), work 2 tog in patt twice, patt 12 (12, 16), work 2 tog in patt twice, patt 6, k1 (selvage)—58 (66, 74) sts.

Row 27: Work even.

Row 28: K1 (selvage), patt 5, work 2 tog twice, patt 10 (10, 14), work 2 tog twice, patt 10 (18, 18), work 2 tog twice, patt 10 (10, 14), work 2 tog twice, patt 5, k1 (selvage)—50 (58, 66) sts.

Row 29: Work even.

Row 30: K1 (selvage), patt 4, work 2 tog twice, patt 8 (8, 12), work 2 tog twice, patt 8 (16, 16), work 2 tog twice, patt 8 (8, 12), work 2 tog twice, patt 4, k1 (selvage)—42 (50, 58) sts.

Row 31: K1 (selvage), patt 3, work 2 tog twice, patt 6 (6, 10), work 2 tog twice, patt 6 (14, 14), work 2 tog twice, patt 6 (6, 10), work 2 tog twice, patt 3, k1 (selvage)—34 (42, 50) sts.

Rows 32 to 35: Work these rows even in check patt.

Row 36: K1 (selvage), patt 6, work 2 tog twice, patt 4 (8, 12), work 2 tog twice, patt 4 (8, 12), work 2 tog twice, patt 6, k1 (selvage)—28 (36, 44) sts.

Row 37: Patt even.

Row 38: K1 (selvage), patt 5, work 2 tog twice, patt 2 (6, 10), work 2 tog twice, patt 2 (6, 10), work 2 tog twice, patt 5, k1 (selvage)—22 (30, 38) sts.

Row 39: Work even.

Row 40: K1 (selvage), patt 4, work 2 tog twice, patt 0 (4, 8), work 2 tog twice, patt 0 (4, 8), work 2 tog twice, patt 4, k1 (selvage)—16 (24, 32) sts. For S size, skip ahead to finishing.

> ## tip
> Maintaining the check patt while shaping the crown requires counting and some concentration. If this isn't for you, try going down a needle size and shaping crown in st st only—I made one that way as a baby gift, and it was very cute.

Row 41—M (L): K1 (selvage), patt 3, work 2 tog twice, patt 2 (6), work 2 tog twice, patt 2 (6), work 2 tog twice, patt 3, k1 (selvage)—18 (26) sts.

Rows 42 to 44: Work even in check patt.

Row 45—M only: K1 (selvage), patt 1, *work 2 tog, patt 2*, rep from * to * three times, with last 2 sts of rep as patt 1, k1 (selvage)—14 sts.

Row 45—L only: Work even in check patt. For M size, skip ahead to finishing.

Row 46—L only: K1 (selvage), patt 6, work 2 tog twice, patt 4, work 2 tog twice, patt 6, k1 (selvage)—22 sts.

Row 47: Work even.

Row 48: K1 (selvage), patt 5, work 2 tog twice, patt 2, work 2 tog twice, patt 5, k1 (selvage)—18 sts.

Row 49: Work even.

Row 50: K1 (selvage), patt 4, work 2 tog four times, patt 4, k1 (selvage)—14 sts.

Finishing
Break yarn, leaving a tail to sew back seam, pull through rem 16 (14, 14) sts, and tighten. Weave in loose ends. Sew back seam, reversing and using B for rolled brim.

Tassel
Cut a 3-in. piece of cardboard. Take a 60-in. length of yarn B, and wrap around cardboard about 20 times. Cut end. With yarn still wrapped around cardboard, take another 40-in. strand of B, and pull through the bottom edge bet cardboard and wrapped strands. Tie it tightly in a knot to secure bottom of tassel. Now insert scissors into the top edge bet the cardboard and wrapped strands, and cut to free the tassel from the cardboard. Cut another short length of B, and tie it around the strands about ¾ in. above the tail. Pull the ends of this piece into the strands of the tassel to hide them, and cut to same length as tassel strands. Using the double strands of the tail, work chain st with crochet hook from base of tassel for about 2 in. Use the rest of the tail to sew tassel to the point of the hat.

RESOURCES

The following yarn suppliers sell wholesale only, but you can contact them to find a retailer or mail-order source in your area.

Alice Starmore Yarns
Distributed by Unicorn Books & Crafts
1338 Ross St.
Petaluma, CA 94954

Brown Sheep Co.
100662 County Road 16
Mitchell, NE 69357

Cascade Yarns
P. O. Box 58168
Tukwila, WA 98138

Classic Elite Yarns
300A Jackson St.
Lowell, MA 01852

Crystal Palace Yarns
3006 San Pablo Ave.
Berkeley, CA 94702

Dale of Norway, Inc.
N16 W23390 Stoneridge Drive
Suite A
Waukesha, WI 53188

Filatura di Crosa
Distributed by Stacey Charles
1061 Manhattan Ave.
Brooklyn, NY 11222

Jo Sharp Yarns
Distributed by Classic Elite Yarns

Muench Yarns
285 Bel Marin Keys
Unit J
Novato, CA 94949

Peace Fleece
475 Porterfield Road
Porter, ME 04068

Rowan Yarns
Distributed by Westminster Fibers
5 Northern Blvd.
Amherst, NH 03031

For Monkeysuits kits or for a list of retail shops that carry Monkeysuits patterns, visit the Monkeysuits website at www.monkeysuits.com, or write:

Monkeysuits
542 Lorimer St., #6
Brooklyn, NY 11211

FURTHER READING

I have found the following knitting instruction books helpful:

Hiatt, June. *The Principles of Knitting: Methods and Techniques of Hand Knitting*. New York: Simon & Schuster, 1988.

Square, Vicki. *The Knitter's Companion*. Loveland, CO: Interweave Press, 1996.

Threads Editors. *Knitting Tips & Trade Secrets*. Newtown, CT: The Taunton Press, 1996.

Vogue Knitting Editors. *Vogue Knitting*. New York: Pantheon Books, 1989.